Africa's Powerhouse

Africa's Powerhouse

The South African Economy: A Pictorial Ensemble

Published by
African International Publishing Company (Pty) Ltd.
Sandton, South Africa.

Printed and bound in the Netherlands
for the publisher African International Publishing Co. (Pty) Ltd.
Sandton, Transvaal, South Africa.

CONTENTS

Cover photograph: Vaal Industry Power Station

INTRODUCTION

For two slow-pulsed centuries time trickled quietly across the vast space of Southern Africa, beyond the small but infinitely symbolic development of Jan van Riebeeck's ship-victualling vegetable garden, beyond even the reckless courage of a handful of people venturing out to print their footsteps across the face of the unknown interior.

The land south of the Limpopo still slept its millenary sleep, with but a brief spasm of burgeoning change here and there. Nearly two hundred years after Van Riebeeck first planted his garden in 1652, hunters and explorers were still using the stars to navigate their wagons across the sea of grass, bigger than the State of Texas, which washed endlessly over the South African Highveld.

The hunters and explorers were often farmers. But the pastoral pattern of their lives hastened neither the pace nor a change in the face of slow drifting time. Then, like the first nascent spark of a bush fire, came a moment of imponderable portent. In the year 1886 an itinerant handyman and prospector made an affidavit, stating simply: ". . . I think I have found a payable gold field."

He had done more than discover gold. He had discovered the key which would unlock the door to South Africa's vast industrial potential, to its treasure-trove of mineral wealth, to the development of the land into a modern nation state which would lead all Africa in technological and economic advancement.

Since that glittering day in 1886, the Witwatersrand Basin has not only produced about 40 per cent of all the gold ever mined in the world but it also provided an essential economic infrastructure and stimulus which would lead to the creation of a modern industrial, urbanised nation in an area covering one and a quarter million square kilometres and providing a home for some twenty-three million of its various peoples.

The transformation did not occur overnight. At first the pace was still pastoral. However, two world wars and their demands on the resources of the country, their prodding influence towards greater economic self-sufficiency, were major factors accelerating development in almost every sector.

Now, over the past 20 years, industrial and technological advancement has reached a crescendo of activity. In this period South Africa has become the workshop of the African continent, accounting for 40 per cent of its entire industrial production. It is the nation with the largest mineral deposits in Africa, more steel and power than the continent as a whole, and is the only region which can produce enough food for all its people. It possesses more tarred roads than all the rest of Africa put together, and owns over half of Africa's total of vehicles and telephones. Its people of all races enjoy the biggest employment opportunities and highest literacy rates on the entire continent.

Urban and regional development are far in advance of anywhere else in Africa. The golden city of Johannesburg, youngest and biggest, is the hub of mining and finance, with a rapidly increasing population of 1,5 million. In area it has doubled in size in 10 years and it is a major catalyst for accelerated industrial and commercial development both in the Transvaal and in the country generally.

The Province of Natal, its green cascading beauty and tropic-like Indian Ocean beaches almost concealing its immense economic potential under a lush, paradisical landscape, is now leading in South African economic growth. Registered factories there have doubled in the past 10 years and the rapid trend of increase continues. Its major city, Durban, is not only one of South Africa's leading industrial centres, but is Africa's busiest port with a cargo-handling growth of nearly 10 per cent a year

In Natal, too, is based a \$750 million sugar industry, and one of the largest and most visionary development projects Africa has yet seen – the creation of an entirely new and vast port-industrial complex at Richards Bay, almost in the hoofprints of the White rhino which reign in the immense game sanctuaries close at hand.

What is virtually virgin land on the historic north coast of Natal is in the process of being transformed into one of Africa's most important new ports and cities, with 1 200 hectares destined for general industrial development – bigger even than Natal's largest existing industrial centre. A vast petro-chemical complex will occupy a similar area. The port area eventually will be capable of handling ships up to 250 000 tons, and will become a bustling gateway through which much of South Africa's mineral wealth will be poured out to the waiting world. An ultra-modern commercial centre will form the urban hub for new residential developments which are expected to accomodate 100 000 people within the next two decades, expanding to 800 000 early in the next century.

Parallel with Natal's industrial expansion is the development of its vast water resources, sufficient to meet the infrastructural needs of a population twice that of South Africa as a whole. The Tugela-Vaal project – incorporating novel hydrological design concepts – is aimed at boosting supplies for the massively expanding industrial complex of the Witwatersrand, while a major programme of dam construction is in progress throughout Natal.

Indicative of Natal's water resource potential are the initial results of a special survey of the Tugela Basin, which shows that a series of dams there could generate more hydro-electric power than even the giant Cabora Bassa.

In South Africa's oldest province, the enchanting history-veined Cape, the patina of an antique land has become burnished with a blend of tranquil landscape and new dynamism of economic progress. Here is sited, for instance, one of the nation's most adventurous development projects – the Saldanha-Sishen scheme involving major mining, railroad and harbour schemes. Well within the current decade Saldanha will provide facilities for ocean-going giants which will bear away raw and processed minerals worth more than \$500 million each year. Total cost of the project will also be nearly \$500 million and many European nations are involved in the undertaking.

A forerunner of schemes on the current huge scale, now in process of development and startling in the breadth and vision of its concept, was the Orange River Project aimed at harnessing the nation's biggest river. Costing \$1 400 million, the scheme has reached an advanced stage; the massive Hendrik Verwoerd Dam is already complete, and constitutes a major phase of a series of three dams in the scheme for irrigation and the generation of hydro-electric power.

In the conception and creation of these large-scale development projects – immense and impressive by any standards, anywhere in the world – South Africa's planning has been focused to a vital extent on the utilisation of its mineral resources. During the two centuries which followed the digging of Van Riebeeck's garden, agriculture was the fulcrum of economic activity. It was the discovery of gold, then diamonds, which triggered a new trend in which the country's mineral riches gained increasing economic predominance. Discovery of new deposits started with a trickle and swelled into a deluge. It began to dawn on South Africa – and on the world at large – that, indeed, this land at the tip of Africa was a veritable treasure chest.

Here lie the world's largest deposits of gold and chrome. Here, too, are probably the largest deposits of platinum group metals, manganese and vanadium. Together with South West Africa it has the largest gem diamond deposits. As if this wasn't enough, South Africa has been bestowed with some of the largest known reserves of uranium, asbestos, high-grade iron ore, antimony, vermiculite and fluorspar. And it possesses Africa's largest known deposits of nickel and titanium. Some 20 metallic and 30 non-metallic minerals are mined – almost all minerals required by modern industry can be found in South Africa, which also has the largest deposits in the whole of the African Continent. It has been officially estimated that mineral exports will rocket by more than six times within the next 25 years, from about \$90 million a year to \$600 million. However, current world market levels suggest that even this increase may be a considerable underestimate.

Over 680 000 workers are employed in the mining industry, and about two out of every three work on gold mines. While the economic importance of other minerals is rapidly increasing, gold mining still remains the most vital mining activity and its product is as equally vital to the world economy. About 75 per cent of the world's newly-mined gold comes annually from South Africa. Out of about 50 large mines, the top 12 produce between them more than half the total output of some 900 metric tons. Some mines produce singly more gold in a year than the entire gold mining industry of the United States. Yet it is believed that more gold still remains to be mined in the Highveld than has yet been extracted.

South Africa is heading for yet another bonanza! The iron and steel industry will probably grow faster than any other mineral industry in South Africa. About 75 per cent of the steel is produced by the State-controlled South African Iron and Steel Industrial Corporation (ISCOR), which is already implementing big expansion schemes in conjunction with smaller producers amounting to nearly \$4 500 million. This does not include some \$700 million to be spent on its Sishen-Saldanha ore export project. ISCOR's expansion plans alone have as their target a production of about 10,5 million tons of raw steel a year by 1983.

The steel industry is based on massive high-quality iron ore reserves. Of known world reserves, at a 60 per cent content, South Africa possesses six per cent, or 5 000 million metric tons. Known reserves containing 25-40 per cent iron are six billion tons. South African producers plan to supply 2,1 per cent of world needs, which by 1990 will mean exporting 46 million metric tons annually.

Known reserves of copper, one of the country's three most important minerals, amount to five million metric tons. World demand is assured. By 1980, production is expected to reach 300 000 metric tons, compared to the 1972 production of 162 000 tons. Manganese reserves are the largest in the world, totalling 2 000 million tons, which is ten times greater than those known in Russia. Output is likely to reach 5,5 million tons by 1980, compared with 3,3 million tons in 1972. About 68 per cent of proven world chrome deposits are to be found in South Africa, with a projected output of 2,2 million tons by the start of the next decade. The world's largest source of vanadium – used in the production of high-quality steel – is in South Africa, which is now supplying the industries of western countries with most of the vanadium they need. Planned expansion of nickel production will result in South Africa providing about six per cent of the world's nickel production.

While huge mineral deposits exist in the nation's predominantly White areas, the Black homelands, now emerging into a new era of national independence and which comprise nearly 14 per cent of South Africa, actually have an even greater potential for mineral discoveries and exploration than the rest of the country. In spite of this potential, little has so far been spent on exploration. In the Bophuthatswana homeland, search for kimberlite pipes and fissures have been successful. Promising geochemical results for copper, zinc, and lead indicate extensive mineralisation. In the Lebowa homeland, test drilling has proved the existence of hundreds of millions of tons of chrome ore. All approaches for prospecting in the homelands by private concerns are channelled through the Bantu Mining Corporation.

An escalating world energy crisis is focusing attention increasingly on those natural resources of a nation which promise to contribute significantly to a solution of this critical problem. Few non-oil producing countries are as fortunate in this respect as South Africa, which utilises oil to meet a mere 20 per cent of its energy needs – compared with 66 per cent for Western Europe and 75 per cent for Japan. South Africa has planned its development on the assumption that the country would become only marginally more dependent on oil within the next six years, with a diminishing percentage reliance on oil from then to the end of the century. The current world energy situation, however, is likely to accelerate the swing away from oil.

It is on coal that South Africa depends to meet nearly 80 per cent of its energy needs – coal at one of the lowest pithead prices in the world. Almost all its electricity is generated from coal, and viable reserves are probably between 12 000 and 20 000 million tons, with still more deposits likely to be discovered. This constitutes nearly 2 per cent of the world's known resources, and by far the biggest deposits in the whole of Africa. Over 60 collieries produce a total of some 60 million tons annually, and this amount is expected to rise to 130 million tons within the next 15 years. Big increases in coal exports are scheduled from 1976, when the new bulk-handling harbour at Richards Bay will be in operation. Through coal-generated power the Electricity Supply Commission, after 20 years of extraordinary growth, implemented its grand strategy in 1974 by which every economically-active region in South Africa would be blanketed by the national grid. Coal is also supplying a proportion of the country's petroleum needs: South Africa is the world's undisputed leader in the technology of producing oil from coal. This highly successful sector is now heading into an exciting future, both as a manufacturer of liquid fuels and gas from coal, and as an exporter of expertise.

Despite the availability of huge coal-derived energy resources, one energy source above all has fired the imagination and hopes of South Africans as a result of brilliant research by their scientists on the ultimate in high output/low volume fuels for nuclear energy, uranium. It occurs in the extensive gold-bearing conglomerates of the Witwatersrand Basin, and the gold fields there constitute one of the largest uranium ore reserves in the western

world, estimated at 300 000 tons. A new route to uranium enrichment, holding decided advantages over existing techniques – it is also about 30 per cent cheaper than existing methods – has been pioneered in South Africa. As a result of this advance, South Africa is building its own $800 million full-scale enrichment plant. This will be completed in the 1980s, and will be able to produce 2 400 tons of enriched uranium annually for domestic use and export from 12 000 tons of uranium oxide coming from the mines. The projected growth in world demand for uranium oxide – rising from about 20 000 tons to between 73 000 and 106 000 tons in 1980, and perhaps 200 000 tons by the year 2000 – justifies South African hopes for a greatly expanded market.

As in its trend towards processing uranium ore to its more advanced stages, South Africa's aim is to produce finished products from her minerals to an increasing degree. The immediate future will see a growth in the export of beneficiated ores and minerals, which can earn far more than unprocessed raw materials. Already certain sectors, such as the ferro-alloy and ferro-chrome industries, are beneficiating a proportion of their product.

Although in the primary product "stakes" the traditional backbone of the economy, agriculture, has been overtaken by the mining industry as far as contribution to the gross domestic product is concerned, the farming industry remains a massive and vital sector of the national economy. Next to gold, it is the most important factor in the country's exports. Sugar exports alone have twice in recent years exceeded one million tons and sugar is now among the top earners of foreign exchange in the sector.

Together with maize, another important export commodity, South African sugar has an international reputation for its quality. Maize production has increased on average by more than one-third over the past 10 years. This growth is expected to continue and it has been estimated that by 1980 average annual production will reach 12 million tons – a 67 per cent rise. Wheat is in surplus production. Deciduous fruit farmers alone earned $80 million from exports in 1973, while South African wines have become increasingly in demand. Livestock production potential is immense: increasing interest in beef production promises to create a lucrative export market, while traditional wool exports brought nearly $250 million during the 1972-73 season. There is potential, too, for a vast production increase in a wide range of crops eagerly sought on world markets, such as cotton and soyabean. A pattern of growth and increasing efficiency occurs over most agricultural sectors. The mechanisation trend on South African farms during the past decade has been even more rapid than that in the United States. Investment in farm plant, implements and vehicles has now reached $200 million a year. With only six per cent of Africa's total land area, South Africa produces over 20 per cent of the continent's total agricultural output.

As a result of the efforts of over 100 000 farmers and 1,5 million workers of all race groups, farming some 110 million hectares, the over-all nutritional level in South Africa is high on the international list. In recent years the per capita daily protein intake has increased from 76 to 88 grams, and calories from 2 700 to 3 200. It is, in fact, the only country in the whole of Africa which is producing enough food for its people. Much of the rest of Africa is being fed by a few developed industrial nations – and when the aid fails to materialise hundreds of thousands, even millions, of human beings die. "The growth of agriculture and food production", says the Food and Agriculture Organisation in its annual report, "is not keeping pace with population increase . . ."

In its 1971 report the FAO pointed out that in 16 out of 39 African countries, per capita agricultural production was actually below the 1961-65 average, and that only seven out of these 16 countries had reached this average level since 1965. At a time of increasing international concern on the recent levels of world grain stocks, aside from an even longer-standing shortage of animal proteins, even the currently inadequate food-aid effort appears to have a bleak future. In situations such as this, it is not altogether surprising that some of South Africa's most bitter critics among the Black States are among the first to seek imports of South African-produced foodstuffs. They are not turned away.

Increasing malnutrition and outright starvation, however, are not conducive to the creation of stable societies, or permit the desperately needed human and economic development. Consequently, it is not surprising that in addition to the high mortality rates now being experienced in many regions of Africa as a direct result of famine and starvation, many more human beings die violently – in social and political upheavals. In addition, it has been estimated that over the past 20 years more than 4,3 million people in Africa have become refugees as a result of famine or political upheavals.

In the absence of a startling – and improbable – upsurge in agricultural technology and volume of production in the African States, it would seem that South Africa's potential role as a larder and granary for many of them could well be realised within the next decade.

Based on the agricultural sector is a rapidly expanding food industry, growing at a rate of between 8 per cent and 10 per cent a year. Even when projections for it are made solely on domestic demand – to be dramatically influenced by a population increase of 246 per cent by the turn of the century – the future looks exceptionally bright.

Manufacturers and processors in this sector know their supply base of raw materials is firm and capable of meeting the challenge for growth. Already 48 per cent of total agricultural production flows to the secondary industry.

The emergence of the secondary sector, surfing impressively on the tide of industrialisation which has made South Africa responsible for about 40 per cent of Africa's total industrial production, has created immense opportunities. By the end of 1973 manufacturing output was 14 per cent higher than the previous year; retail and wholesale sales were showing a 20 per cent advance.

A major factor in this spectacular rate of growth continues to be the increasing purchasing power of South Africa's Non-White population. Among the Bantu (Black) group alone there are now over six million economically active. In recent years their purchasing power was boosted by wide-ranging wage increases varying from 20 to 40 per cent. At a real growth in the South African economy of an attainable six per cent, the projected income of the Non-White race groups within the next 25 years should account for more than 40 per cent of national income. The impact of this trend on the domestic market is already obvious. From out of Johannesburg's Black township of Soweto alone, the annual consumer power expended in shops amounts to more than $750 million. And the country's total population is still growing at the rate of almost one a minute, or half a million a year.

But South Africans, of all races, are not merely consumers. They are workers and, above all, they are people. In 1925 when industrialisation in South Africa was in its birth pangs, there were a mere 60 000 Black workers employed in factories. Today there are well over a million. They represent about 40 per cent of the total employment in industry, the rest being shared by Whites, Coloureds (people of mixed descent) and Asians. The conditions of employments of all groups have undergone immense improvement as the economy developed; and this entails not only a rapid increase in job opportunities based on potential economic growth, but the affording of new opportunities for education and worker-training. Without these the essential levels of production are unattainable. Recognition of this has resulted in a major expansion in education programmes.

The number of Black children alone now attending school is approaching the four million mark – 90 per cent. Government-subsidised training centres for Black workers and subsidised in-plant training schemes are being launched in all the main industrial centres. The greater use of this trained non-White labour has been officially accepted as a pre-requisite to the achievement of an adequate economic growth rate and to the creation of sufficient job opportunities. Industrial production in Natal, for instance, is expected to double within the next 10 years with employment doubling every 15 years.

A concept of economic growth, however, becomes a mere academic exercise if divorced from the human factors involved in a country's effort to advance. Industrial relations and employer-worker communication are essential ingredients in both productivity and community accord. When a variety of race groups, frequently with language barriers, are involved in the same enterprise, adequate machinery to achieve such communication becomes even more indispensible. South Africa does not believe that trade unionism in the European pattern can secure these goals. Cultural and developmental differences would annul even the more desirable features of the trade union structure which had been transplanted directly from a totally dissimilar cultural and social environment. Machinery for industrial negotiations must, in effect, evolve out of the particular situation and environment of the worker-group itself. Consequently, South Africa has opted for a system of works committees, and already many of these are formulating strategies out of their own experience which augur well for the development of composite machinery which will be both equitable and effective. Meanwhile, South Africa recognises the need for a pragmatic, open-minded approach to this facet of industrial and human development, but it wants to "do its own thing" in its own time and in its own way. Justification for this approach is self-evident. Fewer labour disputes and less person-to-person disharmony occur in South African industry than in any other comparable national industry.

The entire spectrum of industry and of those who man it is supported by substantial development and research resources, spearheaded by the national research institutions of the Council for Scientific and Industrial Research. It is also serviced by the most sophisticated and respected banking system in Africa.

Commercial banking commenced in South Africa in 1793 with the establishment of the Lombard Bank under the auspices of the Dutch East India Company. A steady tempo of growth down the centuries was suddenly accelerated after World War II when the number of commercial banks nearly doubled as a result of foreign banks launching subsidiaries and associate companies. Now South Africa has over 50 registered banking institutions, including both commercial and merchant banks. The first merchant bank was Union Acceptances, established by the Anglo American Corporation Ltd., in conjunction with Lazard Bros. and Co. Ltd., in 1955. It was joined by the establishment of a number of other merchant banks, many with direct links with counterparts in Britain. By 1963, an official Technical Committee decided that as merchant banks had an important role as credit-creators they should come under the control of the Central Bank. Total assets of these banks by 1973 amounted to nearly $1 400 million.

Government policy towards the banking structure generally has been stated categorically: no nationalisation. Even the special provisions which it has laid down regarding shareholdings in banks because of their economically strategic activities is relatively minimal. The character of the South African banking system is, therefore, far different to that found in many other parts of Africa.

This is also reflected in the nature of the South African Reserve Bank, which was established over 50 years ago. At the centre of the nation's economy, the bank has played a skilled and impressive role in the surging industrial development of what was not long ago a predominantly pastoral region. It markets the gold output, a highly complex operation, and conducts a large part of South Africa's international economic relationships.

A leading role is played by South African banking in what is internationally recognised as one of the best investment fields in the world. Investment interest in South Africa is obviously influenced by the level of interest rates elsewhere. In effect, by experiencing a relatively low rate of inflation and accompanying moderate interest rates, South Africa occasionally sees some investment diverted to countries with high rates of both interest and inflation. This does not unduly perturb the South African financial authorities, as they regard this as merely a transitory phase in an investment cycle, in which the recognition of the value-for-money quality of investment in South Africa is ultimately the more powerful influence. An additional aspect of the intrinsic attractiveness of South African investment is the lack of restrictive legislation, such as is now common in many other countries traditionally regarded as investment areas. Most nations, for instance, now legislate about foreign ownership of the equity of their industries – some insisting that 51 per cent or more of the shares should be held by local institutions. In contrast, South Africa says that investments are doubly welcome if made in partnership with South African shareholders, but this is definitely not a pre-condition. South Africa welcomes foreign investment, particularly when accompanied by technological expertise and skilled workers, and its treatment of foreign investors as far as taxation is concerned is recognised world-wide as being especially fair.

A facet of the investment field which is increasing in importance is that of industrial development in the Black homelands. Substantial government assistance is afforded entrepreneurs who establish concerns in these areas, including formidable concessions to exporters. Incentives follow a similar pattern to that found in the regional development policies of several European countries, and are channelled through the Bantu Investment Corporation. An upsurge of interest is being shown by industrialists in this field, and a number of overseas' companies are already establishing enterprises in the homelands. A prominent non-financial attraction is the abundance of labour.

World recognition of the investment potential of South Africa has had considerable reinforcement in recent years from national and international economic trends. Lack of economic and social stability over large areas of the world has accentuated the solid foundations of the South African economy. The world's worsening energy situation has highlighted both South Africa's wealth in alternative energy resources – coal and uranium – as well as its comparatively small dependence on oil as an energy source for its own industrial sector. Even in the case of oil-derivatives, South Africa can rely largely on coal-based raw materials for substitution. As a source of vital raw materials, both mineral and non-mineral, South Africa becomes ever more significant. In addition, there is gold and its continuing crucial role both in the world monetary system and in the adjustment of the domestic economy of South Africa.

There is every indication that South Africa is on the threshold of a new period of strong economic expansion. This widely-held conviction is based not only on the country's material and physical resources, but also on its human resources. A large, eager labour force has recently boosted its productivity per man-hour in industry by 4,7 per cent, and with a large educational and training programme in operation productivity should rise still faster in the future.

When Van Riebeeck in 1652 first set his men to dig a garden in the Cape, he could hardly have foreseen that he was initiating a chain of development, both human and material, which has gathered momentum ever since. But at no subsequent period in the nation's history has such a degree of acceleration, both in effort and achievement, occurred as at the present time. And this is supremely evident in South Africa's goal of full development for all its people, of whatever race they may be. This aspect of development calls for an objectively conscious effort backed by material and economic advancement. Nowhere in the world can such development be regarded as an inevitable process, a leisurely march to a well signposted goal. It demands hard, sustained endeavour and a determination to utilise a nation's natural resources to bring enrichment in its widest meaning to the lives of all its people.

The South African challenge is surely also the most exciting of any nation, for it has made South Africa the living workshop in which human relationships, as well as economic destinies, are being hammered out with such decisive implications for the future – not only for South Africa but for the hopes of men everywhere.

A profile of the South African economy appears at the back of this book covering infrastructure, population and national income, banking and financial institutions, foreign investment, trade, natural resources, mining and manufacturing, agriculture, labour, economic policy and aid to Africa.

THE EDITORS

INDUSTRY

For all practical purposes, South Africa is the only producer of steel on the African continent. The South African Iron and Steel Industrial Corporation (ISCOR) contributes well over three-quarters of the Republic's steel output. The photograph shows ISCOR's Pretoria works.

Photo: ISCOR

The temper mill for the electrolytic tinning line at the Vanderbijlpark Works of the South African Iron and Steel Corporation (ISCOR). Slab and plate production at the mill are computer-assisted, while an X-ray gauge is incorporated to measure the thickness of the plate being rolled.

Photo: ISCOR

A Bo-bo Electric locomotive 3 200 HP operating on 3 000 volts ready for delivery to the South African Railways. It was manufactured by Union Carriage, one of the world's largest rolling stock manufacturers. The other photo shows rolling stock under manufacture at the company's Nigel works.

Photo: Union Carriage

The world's most powerful mine winder. The winder was manufactured in South Africa for the No. 2 shaft at the East Driefontein gold mine near Carletonville. The four drums are driven by two motors, each designed to hoist 18,5 metric tons from a maximum depth of 2 018 metres at a speed of 1 098 metres per minute.

Photo : VECOR

A basic oxygen furnace being charged at the Highveld
Steel and Vanadium Works at Witbank in the
Transvaal.

Photo: Anglo American Corporation

A metallurgist of the South African Bureau of
Standards inspecting a heavy gear wheel blank
intended for a steel rolling mill in Britain – he is
testing the hardness of the rim on which gear
teeth will be cut.

Photo: SABS

Casting a 95-ton mill housing
intended for a South African
steel works.

Photo: VECOR

The walking beam furnace at the Scaw Metals Works' merchant rod and bar mill discharging a white-hot steel block. Because of the plentiful deposits of high-grade iron-ore, the price of basic iron and steel in South Africa is well below that of most countries in the Western world.

Photo: Anglo American Corporation

19

Ingot casting in progress at the Southern Cross Steel Company works, near Middleburg in the Transvaal. The company forms part of a group of companies manufacturing stainless steel and ferro-chromium alloys for export and domestic consumption. Southern Africa possesses about 80 per cent of the world's known reserves of chrome ores.

Photo: Barlow Rand group

This aluminium factory at Pietermaritzburg in Natal manufactures a large variety of products, such as sheeting and foil. Use of this metal in South Africa has increased by 18 per cent in the last 10 years in comparison with eight per cent in the rest of the world. A new smelter erected at Richards Bay on the Natal coast will eliminate the need to import aluminium ingots.

Photo: Alcan Ltd.

The physical ruggedness of the country is a never-ending
challenge to the local engineering and construction industry.
The picture shows the Van Staden's Gorge bridge under
construction in 1970.

Photo: Johannesburg Consolidated Investment Co.

Good housing, schools, pay, climate and wide open spaces attract thousands of skilled workers from Europe every year. In the past decade 450 000 immigrants came to South Africa.

Photo: S. Robertson

A modern, open-hearth, electric submerged arc furnace at Rand Carbide. The furnace produced ferro-silicon from iron shavings and quartzite, with coal char as the reductant. Ferro-silicon is one of the number of ferro-alloys being produced in the Eastern Transvaal. They are used by the associated steel alloy industries for the production of the ever more sophisticated materials called for by advancing engineering technology.

Photo: Shell Company of S.A. Ltd.

Night scene at Sasol, the South African Coal, Oil and Gas
Corporation's plant, some 70 kilometres south of Johannesburg.
This unique factory – the largest commercial oil-from-coal
plant in the world – converts low-grade coal into oil, gas and
chemical by-products. It has also resulted in South Africa
becoming an exporter of a variety of organic chemicals.

Photo: Struan Robertson

A 1,07 metre by 1,65 metre Allis-Chalmers superior gyratory crusher manufactured for the Federale Mynbou's Buffalo Fluorspar mine at Naboomspruit by Vecor Vanderbijl Park.

Photo: VECOR

In 1970 it was announced that South African scientists had developed a new uranium enrichment process. By 1973 a pilot plant had been built at Pelindaba, near Pretoria (photo below). More than 90 per cent of the material for the plant was locally manufactured – involving some 235 firms. The other photo shows the interior of the plant's services building.

Photos: Perskor

A night scene of South African Polyolefins Limited's polymerisation plant at Sasolburg. The plant was constructed in the light of the rapidly developing market for high density polyethylene and the availability of the raw material ethylene.

Photo: Sentrachem

In 1971 South Africa's first inland oil refinery was inaugurated at Sassolburg in the Orange Free State. The Natref (National Petroleum Refiners Ltd.) refinery is a joint enterprise of South Africa's Sasol, the French Company Total and the National Iranian Oil Company. Experts from 12 countries undertook the design of the R70-million project. The photo at bottom left shows the plant's control room.

Photo: S.A. Panorama

Thousands of cylinders lined up ready for filling with "arcton" gas at AE and CI's factory near Sasolburg. The past two decades have seen dramatic growth in the country's chemical industry. Capital investment now exceeds R1 000 million and products worth more than R600 million are manufactured annually, making the chemical industry the fourth largest industrial group in South Africa. Within the next decade, the Republic expects to produce locally all the heavy chemicals she requires.

Photo: AE & CI

Exhibits illustrating South Africa's sophisticated jewellery trade. The craft is controlled by a trade union and strict standards are laid down for training, production and ethics. A Jewellery Council, controls the supply and marketing of the finished product. Pictured above left are earings, ring and 22 carat gold bracelet with different coloured tourmalines.
Top right: A floral spray of deep yellow and other delicately coloured diamonds, one of a pair of earrings. Below is a gold brooch studded with brilliants. Most of the diamonds used originate in South Africa. Sales of these precious stones realise more than R90 million annually.

Photos: Chamber of Mines, Anglo American Corporation

The 15 000-ton oil rig, Sedco 135 arrives in Table Bay (Cape
Town) before commencing her task of drilling for oil off the
South African coast. Despite its great variety of mineral riches,
South Africa has not yet found oil deposits. A Government-
sponsored body, the Southern Oil Exploration Corporation, is
charged with accelerating and intensifying the search for
crude oil and gas.

Photo : Cloete Breytenbach

The South African Manufacturing Company's plant at Reunion,
Durban – the plant produces the base oils from which finished
lubricating oils are blended.

Photo: Shell Company of S.A. Ltd.

The local manufacture of rubber products is currently receiving a strong stimulus from the rapidly expanding economy generally.
Seen here is an aerial view of the SARMCOL Works in Howick, Natal, the largest manufacturer of industrial rubber products in South Africa.
The well-known Howick Falls are in the foreground.

Photo: SARMCOL

Yet another giant earthmover tyre is born! The overhead crane lifts a mould – in which the largest earthmover tyres in South Africa are cured – from one of the huge curing "pots" in the Firestone Port Elizabeth plant. The big dome seen in the background covers three of these moulds during the curing process which takes up to eight hours to complete.

Photo: Firestone, Port Elizabeth

Safripol's polymerisation reactor in which ethylene gas is
converted into high density polyethelyne (HDPE) power.
HDPE resins are widely used in the plastics industry.

Photo: Sentrachem, Johannesburg

The Modderfontein dynamite factory near Johannesburg
(pictured) and its sister factory at Somerset West, in the Cape
Province supply all the explosives requirements of Southern
Africa. Altogether more than 80 different explosives and
13 000 explosives accessories are manufactured.

Photo: AE & CI

A paper and pulp mill near Nelspruit, in the Eastern Transvaal. Since the Second World War, local production of paper and board has increased from 28 000 tons to 550 000 tons, and South Africa now meets about 80 per cent of her requirements.

Photos: Barlow Rand

In real terms, South Africa's economy has grown at
an annual average of nearly 5 per cent over the past
quarter of a century – a remarkable performance by
any standard. This has meant a booming building
and construction industry. The photo shows a
skyscraper accommodation complex going up in the
central area of Johannesburg.

Photo: Africamera

Camera fish-eye view of the R100-million Carlton
Centre. South Africa's largest single building
complex, with a hotel, below ground-level shopping
malls, an exhibition centre large enough to contain
a jumbo jet, and probably the biggest office block in
the country.

Photo: SATOUR

Blocking out the sky are the facades of two of Pretoria's modern buildings. This is the living and working patterns of an increasing number of the administrative capital's half-million inhabitants. More than 400 000 workers of all races are employed in the construction industry. The value of building plans passed average about R850 million for the past decade.

Photo : Raymond Otte

The main production floor of the South African Philips
television and radio factory in Martindale, Johannesburg. In
the foreground are the radio production lines and the newly
installed television production lines are towards the rear of
the factory.

Photo: Philips

Aerial view of the General Motors Manufacturing and Assembly
Plant in Port Elizabeth. Despite its comparatively small
population of about 23 million, South Africa was rated 15th
among car-owning countries in 1971 and 16th in overall vehicle
registrations. By October 1973, 18 vehicle assembly plants
were in operation. Vehicle manufacturers bought components,
materials and other supplies totalling R142 million during the
12 months ended 30th June, 1972. During the same period,
salaries and wages totalled R63 500 000.

Photo: S.A. Digest

42

Aerial view of Fiat S.A.'s Rosslyn assembly plant in Pretoria
taken shortly after its completion in October 1968. Situated on
a 52 acre site, the plant has a production capacity of 15 000
cars and trucks per annum on a single shift.

Photo: Fiat

Fiat 125s nearing completion at Fiat's modern Rosslyn assembly
plant.

Photo: Fiat

The Ridge, a multi-purpose cargo ship built by Dorbyl, ready for launching at Durban. In the picture below a S.A. Bureau of Standards technologist carries out a test on a ship in dry dock at Durban. Shipbuilding has become of national importance since 1963, when the State-appointed Norval Commission recommended the establishment of a large-scale industry centred in Durban.

Photos: Dorbyl and SABS

Fishing boats off the Cape West Coast. The combined fish catch of the inshore pelagic surface shoal fishing industry of the Republic and South West Africa averages more than a million short tons annually. About half of the total production is exported. The registered fishing fleet consists of over 7 000 vessels of which some 1 000 are powered craft, including six whale catches. The total value of capital employed in the inshore sector of the industry exceeds R150 million.

Photo : Chris Jansen

A global view of Siemens low voltage switchgear manufactured in South Africa. Owing to the Republic's great demand for sophisticated communication services, the electronics and telecommunications industry is facing a boom period. A diffusion plant at Boksburg, Transvaal, is producing the first transistors to be made in Africa.

Photo: Lindsay Smithers

A torpedo hot-metal transfer car used by the Vecor Heavy
Engineering Company. The company produces parts for cranes
and crane machinery, turbine castings, boiler drums, sugar
mills, heavy hydraulic presses and coke-oven equipment.

Photo: VECOR

Philips Telecommunications manufactures loading coils for the South African Post Office. These devices are used to boost voice quality in underground telephone cables. About R700 million will be spent by the Post Office over a five-year period on communications networks. Telephone services are already available to about 150 countries.

Photo: Philips

Sophisticated equipment enables the South African textile
industry to compete with overseas manufacturers. Pictured is
the blending of wool fibre in the drawing department at the Hex
River Textile Mills, Worcester – one of the country's seven
wool-textile factories.

Photo: Raymond Otte

An everyday scene at the Good Hope Textile Corporation's textile plant at King William's Town, Eastern Cape. Pictured is part of the roller printing process.

Photo: Good Hope Textile Corporation

South Africa's policy of industrial decentralisation is intimately tied up with its efforts to further the economic development of the ethnic Black homelands. A major part of this development is taking place in the border areas of these territories. Regions within roughly 50 kilometres of the ethnic homelands which, apart from labour, offer locational advantages, can qualify as Border areas. The Republic's reasons for developing the Border areas correspond with internationally accepted reasons for industrial decentralisation. Considerable inducements, including substantial tax concessions, are offered to White industrialists to attract manufacturing industry to these areas. There are already several large industrial complexes situated near the borders of the Black homelands such as Rosslyn, near Pretoria. Pictured is an aerial view of this rapidly expanding growth point.

Photo: S.A. Panorama

Pouring the gold. South Africa's gold mines produce an average of 500 000 fine ounces of gold per week, refined by the Rand Refinery at Germiston. The Reserve Bank sells approximately 70 per cent of the newly-mined gold on the free world markets on behalf of the Republic's mines. South Africa produces more than 77 per cent of the free world's gold. The country's gold sources are co-ordinated by the Chamber of Mines. Altogether 48 gold-mining companies are members of the Chamber.

Pictured on the right is a portion of the Western Deep Levels mining complex on the Far West Rand – the world's deepest mining shaft (3 350 metres) still being worked.

Photos: Chamber of Mines and Anglo American Corporation

A two-stage gas producer in the process of being erected by Dorbyl at Olifantsfontein in the Transvaal. The unit produces gas from bituminous coal and is one of the many such plants supplied to industry throughout the country. With the Republic's large reserves of gas-making coal, and the world talking about an energy crisis, these plants are of great advantage to industry.

Photo: Dorbyl

MINING

Stacks of gold bars at the South African Reserve Bank in Pretoria.
The Republic produces approximately three-quarters of the gold in the Free World.
Gold from the various mines is refined at the Rand Refinery, and prepared for disposal through the Reserve Bank.
By far the greatest proportion is sold overseas.
Gold is refined to a purity of 996 parts gold per 1 000 and cast into bars weighing 12,5 kilograms (400 Troy ounces).

Photo: S.A. Panorama

Blasting in progress at the Palabora open-pit mine, one of the world's largest open-pit copper mines. It is situated on the border of the Kruger National Park in the North Eastern Transvaal. The mine can really be described as a minerals processing plant, so wide is the diversity of minerals and chemicals yielded by the immense body of ore. The phosphate reserves are so vast that South Africa is assured of its phosphate fertilizer requirements for many centuries.

Photo: Shell Company of S.A.

South Africa's reserves of platinum are enormous and will ensure the viability of the country's platinum industry for the foreseeable decades. First, copper and nickel are recovered and then the platinum-group metals and gold are extracted. The photograph shows the reduction works and smelter at the Rustenburg Platinum Mine.

Photo: Johannesburg Consolidated Investment Company

Johannesburg is the headquarters of the South African mining
industry. Over 50 minerals are mined in the Republic. In 1972
minerals worth approximately R2 000-million were sold,
making mining the country's largest industry. In addition to
being one of the world's biggest uranium producers, the
Republic has about 75% of the free world's reserves of
chrome ore and more than 40% of the world's manganese ore.

Photo: David Shirley

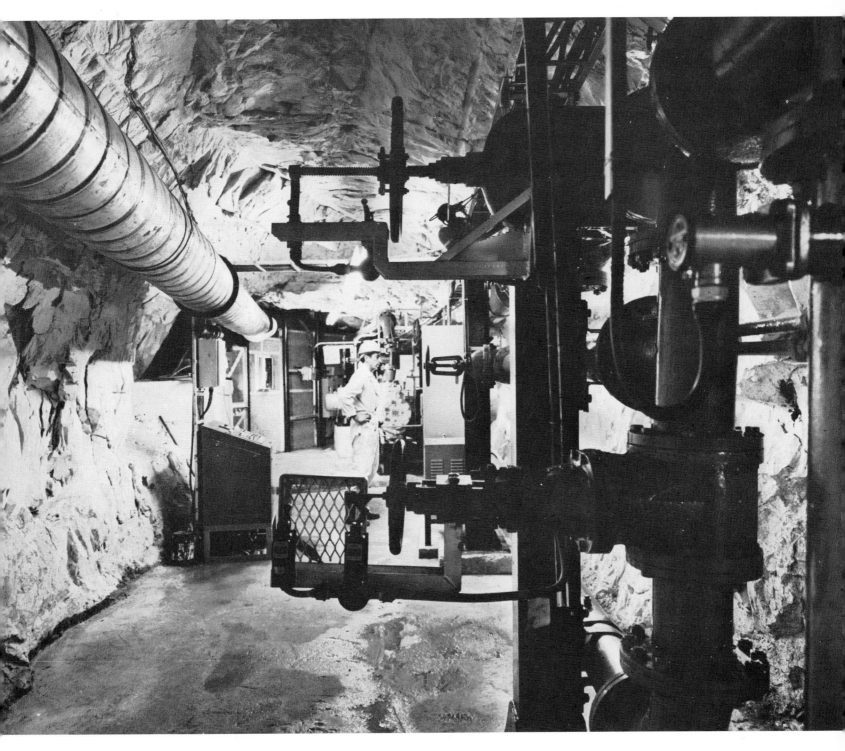

The air receiver control chamber of an Orange Free State gold mine. The intricacy of the problems of cooling and ventilation in deep-level mines is indicated by the fact that rock temperature rises from 65°F. to 123°F. at 11 000 feet (3 352 metres).

Photo: Anglo American Corporation

A panoramic view of the Western Deep Levels gold mine – the deepest mine in the world. In 1974 a depth of more than 3 400 metres was reached, and the mine will ultimately descend to 3 600 metres. South Africa also has the world's largest gold mine, as well as the world's richest gold mine. At the commencement of 1973, some 69 gold mines were in production, of which no less than 50 were classified as large mines (i.e. milling over 20 000 tons of ore a month).

Photo: Anglo American Corporation

South Africa has been called the treasure house of the world because it is so richly endowed with minerals. She has the largest deposits, or ranks among the world's leading producers of gold, diamonds, platinum, uranium, coal, iron ore, manganese, asbestos, chromite, antimony and vanadium. The top photograph shows the Rustenburg Platinum Mines, the world's largest underground mining operation.

In the field of deep-mining techniques, South Africa has no superiors. In the Transvaal, miners first descend a mile to reach sea-level, then continue for a further mile below sea-level. The Photograph shows a White and a Black miner drilling into gold bearing ore.

Photos: Barlow Rand

This mine produces 20 per cent of the world's production of
antimony, a strategic material. It is the Consolidated Murchison
mine, some 350 kilometres north-east of Pretoria. South Africa
is the Free World's largest exporter of this mineral.

Photo: G. Cassel

Most of the salt produced in the Republic is derived from salt pans in the arid inland areas. The supply is sufficient for local consumption. Salt finds its biggest use in the chemical industry in the form of chlorine, caustic soda and soda ash.

Photo: S.A. Panorama

It is estimated that South Africa has over 75 000 million tons of coal deposits. The coal is mined both by way of underground mines and open-cast collieries. The bottom photograph shows a giant walking dragline in action. The dragline weighs over 2 000 tons and can dig to a depth equal to that of a 10-storey building, scooping up 42 cubic metres at every bite.

Photo: Chamber of Mines/Shell Company of S.A.

An electronically operated coal-cutter chews away at the coal
face in an underground mine. South Africa produces 90% of
all coal mined in Africa and her coal reserves represent 80%
of the estimated reserves. New developments include a
R1 000-million project announced in 1974 for the exploitation
of coal fields in the Transvaal, including the construction of a
800 kilometre coal slurry pipeline for large-scale exports.

Photo: S.A. Panorama

Coal speeds to the surface by way of a modern conveyor belt. Large reserves of coal made it feasible to establish the South African Coal, Oil and Gas Corporation (SASOL) – a unique factory producing liquid fuels and a range of chemicals from low grade coal. Coal is therefore playing an important role in helping the Republic to draw closer to self-sufficiency in petroleum products.

Photo: S.A. Panorama

The Republic of South Africa produces more gem diamonds than any other country in the world, and in the production of industrial diamonds she is second only to Zaire. Together with the USA it is the only country manufacturing synthetic diamonds. The picture on the right shows gem diamonds mined at Kimberley. Below a Johannesburg cutter prepares to split a diamond into halves. At the bottom (centre) a diamond tipped saw cuts into a block of granite. On the far right are synthetically produced diamonds.

Photos: S.A. Panorama

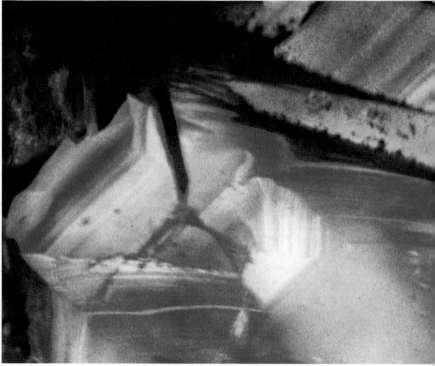

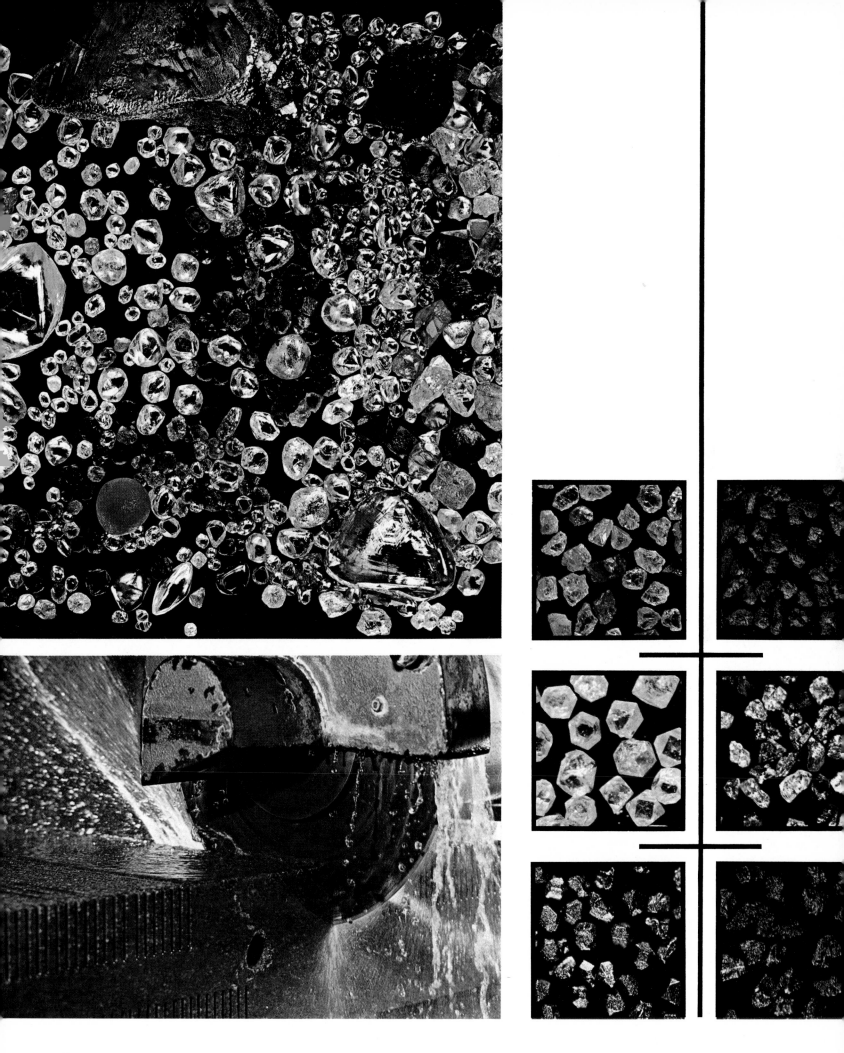

FINANCE & COMMERCE

South Africa's industrial revolution over the past two
decades has spurred the growth of building societies.
Today South Africa ranks fourth in the building
society movement in the world after the USA, Great
Britain and West Germany, with total assets
exceeding $6,74 billion. This striking sculpture is in
the foyer of the headquarters of the United Building
Society in Johannesburg.

Photo: United Building Society

Flat dwellers as well as home owners are indebted to building
societies. A maximum of 15 per cent of building society funds
goes towards the financing of flat complexes – such as this
giant on Durban's foreshore.

Photo: S.A. Panorama

At the apex of the banking and financial pyramid in South Africa is the South African Reserve Bank. It was established in 1920 and is situated in the heart of Pretoria, South Africa's administrative capital. The statue on the left is of Paul Kruger, President of the South African Republic at the turn of the century, when the British Empire fought a bitter war with the Boer Republics.

Photo: S.A. Panorama

At the base of the banking pyramid in South Africa are the commercial banks. There are nine registered commercial banks with over 3 000 branches and agencies throughout the country.
The total assets of the commercial banks have increased from $2,4 billion in 1963 to $7,5 billion in September 1973. The photograph is of the Standard Bank headquarters in Johannesburg. The building was constructed by ''hanging'' the floors from the top, working down to ground level.

Photo: Standard Bank

Johannesburg is the hub of the financial and commercial sectors. It is here that one will find the headquarters of most commercial, general, merchant, savings and hire purchase banks, including the discount and mining houses. In the background are some of the gold mine dumps which have made Johannesburg famous.

Photo: David Shirley, Johannesburg

South Africa, in terms of combined exports and imports, is one of the world's 12 largest trading nations. It follows a strict neutral policy trade with all countries, rejecting any kind of trade boycotts and making facilities available even to those countries who are hostile. Although the Soviet Union is actively supporting an oil embargo against South Africa, her ships continue to visit South African ports. The photograph shows a giant Soviet container vessel taking in bunker oil and supplies in Cape Town harbour.

Photo: Eckley Dykman, Cape Town

South African exports go to more than 100 countries, mostly
Europe, Japan and the United States. Exports vary from
agricultural products to automobile parts. The photograph
shows deciduous fruit being loaded in Cape Town for export
to Britain.

Photo: South African Railways Publicity Office

Africa is a growing market for South African exports, even
to those countries politically hostile to the Republic. A
consignment of heavy-duty conveyor belting is being loaded
for export to the Zambian copper mines.

Photo: Geoff Hunter, Johannesburg

The mining houses of South Africa have been behind some of the most spectacular building projects on the African continent. The 50 storey giant is the Anglo-American Corporation's Carlton Centre project in Johannesburg. The five star Carlton Hotel on the right and skyscraper office block, stand above two levels of underground shopping arcades. The restaurant and pool in the picture (left) are on the first level.

Photo: Carlton Centre

A feature of South African cities today is modern
one-stop shopping centres. The pictures on this
page were taken in Pretoria's Arcadia Centre which
houses approximately 50 shops and air-conditioned
malls.

Photo: S.A. Panorama

Pictures of the Sandton Shopping Centre, situated in Johannesburg's northern suburbs. This complex provides an even greater variety of shopping than New York's famous Rockefeller Centre.

Photo: Sandton Publicity

South Africa's major agricultural, industrial and commercial
exhibition is held in Johannesburg each year over Easter.
The 1974 show featured the world's largest single public
display of gold bullion. Here visitors admire 201 gold bars
worth $7,5 million at the Chamber of Mines' Pavilion.

Photo: S.A. Chamber of Mines

The Johannesburg Stock Exchange was established in 1887. Since then it has been rehoused four times and at present yet another exchange is in the planning stage. Some 500 companies are listed on the exchange as well as approximately 400 government and municipal loan stocks. At the end of 1973 the annual trade in shares exceeded 600 million. The market value of shares in mid-1973 was almost $53 billion, representing 1 405 listed securities and a total issued capital of $17,5 billion.

Photo: Johannesburg Stock Exchange

Municipalities are having to plan well ahead in order
to cater for the growing demands of mushrooming
communities. This is an aerial view of the new
Johannesburg municipal market. Each of the halls
is over 300 metres long.

Photo: Dorbyl, Johannesburg

The hustle and bustle of Johannesburg where some 300 foreign companies are housed continues late into the
night. Here lights burn late in the Schlessinger Centre. Between 1967 and 1973, foreign investors have injected
an average of $700 million per annum into South Africa.

Photo: Business South Africa

The first South African Life Insurance Company came into being in 1845. Today the bulk of life insurance is done by four South African institutions: S.A. Mutual, Sanlam, Southern Life and African Life. The total premium income of all life insurers exceeds $300 million annually. The S.A. Mutual is the largest of the four, with assets totalling $1,7 billion in 1974. The headquarters of this company (pictured) is in Cape Town.

Photo: Terence McNally, Cape Town

Supermarkets are a relatively new feature of
commercial life in South Africa, but recently they
have mushroomed all over the country. This large
supermarket is on the outskirts of the city of
Germiston.

Photo: S.A. Panorama

INFRASTRUCTURE

Like a diamond necklace, the lights of Durban are reflected in
the tranquil waters of the inner harbour. Durban is Africa's
largest port and is located on the south-east coast.

Photo: S.A. Panorama

Cape Town, the Mother City, was founded in 1652 and is the country's second largest port. The harbour is currently being enlarged to double its capacity. The peninsula on which the city is located is the dividing line between the Indian Ocean (on the horizon) and the Atlantic Ocean (foreground). Table Mountain can be seen on the right.

Photo: Protea Colour Prints

Since the closing of the Suez Canal in 1967, thousands of ships have made use of the Cape sea route. On some days 70 to 80 vessels pass the port city of Cape Town. In order to speed up traffic helicopters are used to ferry mail and supplies to passing ships.

Photo: The Sunday Times

The South African Broadcasting
Corporation's television complex
under construction in Johannesburg.
Apart from television the country is
served by an extensive FM network,
and radio broadcasts are conducted
in nine languages for the different
population groups. In addition South
Africa has 700 magazines and
journals, including 23 daily newspapers. This comprises 50 per cent
of all media production in Africa.

Photo: Die Vaderland

The Hertzog radio and television tower
dominates the central Johannesburg skyline. At 269
metres it is the highest man made structure in Africa.

Photo: S.A. Digest

The telecommunications industry has made rapid strides. The first telephone was installed 90 years ago. Today the country has some two million telephones. South African technicians also man and maintain one of two deep space tracking stations near Pretoria. In the picture is the tracking antenna at Hartebeeshoek constructed by the United States. The other station belongs to France.

Photo: Etienne du Plessis and S.A. Panorama

The Blue train, one of the world's most luxurious passenger trains, leaves Cape Town for Johannesburg, approximately 1 600 kilometres away. Table Mountain provides an interesting backdrop. The country has over 22 000 kilometres of railway and the length of electrified track is exceeded only by the USA and Canada. The state-owned South African Railways carries 50 per cent of all freight moved on the African continent.

Photo: South African Railways Publicity Office

Johannesburg's railway station is twice as big as
New York's Grand Central Station. The South African
Railways and Harbours Administration employs
300 000 people and the annual budget exceeds a
billion dollars.

Photo: South African Railways Publicity Office

97

For a rapidly developing industrial state, power is of the
utmost importance. South Africa is fortunate in that she is
dependent on outside sources for only 20 per cent of her
power requirements. This is due largely to the enormous
deposits of coal. Giant power stations are built atop these
coal fields, such as this coal burner at Camden, in the province
of the Transvaal, which generates 1 600 megawatts.

Photo: Electricity Supply Commission and S.A. Panorama

Virtually all of South Africa's electricity is produced by the
Electricity Supply Commission. The country's deposits of coal
lie close to the surface and can be mined at the lowest pit-head
price in the industrial world. Generators of most power
stations are driven by coal burning steam plant. (The first
nuclear power plant will be operational by 1980.) By the end
of 1973 the entire country was hooked up to a central grid.
Here at Simmer Pan is one of the modern control centres.

Photo: Electricity Supply Commission

The power grid which feeds electricity to all parts of South Africa stretches from the coal fields of the Transvaal down to Cape Town as well as to neighbouring African states. The country's unit consumption of electricity per capita currently equals that in Western Europe. The abundance of electricity is borne out by this striking view of the lights of Cape Town stretching for 25 kilometres.

Photo: Herman Geusteyn and Die Burger

The S.A. Vaal (30,212 tons) a
one-class hotel ship, belonging
to SAFMARINE is one of the
seven mail ships carrying
passengers, Mail and cargo
between South Africa and the
United Kingdom.

Photo : CASTLE MARINE

The port of Durban handles
more than 32 million tons of
goods every year. The Bayhead
goods-shed served by a
network of railway lines is
large enough to accommodate
a dozen football fields.

Photo : Alcan Aluminium

With one in ten South Africans owning a car and densely populated urban areas, construction of modern exit roads and freeways have received high priority in the past decade. The country has some 59 000 kilometres of tarred roads. The photographs shows the approach roads to the east coast city of Port Elizabeth.

Photo: S.A. Panorama

103

More than $2 billion will be spent during the next ten years on the expanding of the country's motorway network. The photograph shows a fly-over in Johannesburg.

Photo : Klem Lloyd Lithographers

An aerial view of Saldanha Bay, one of the country's few natural harbours. Here a new deep water port is being constructed as part of the $500 million Saldanha-Sishen scheme (involving major mining and railway projects). Within the next few years Saldanha will provide berths for super tankers of 300 000 tons including dry dock facilities. In eight years time it is expected that mineral and processed exports worth between $450-500 million per year will flow from Saldanha.

Photo: S.A. Panorama

At Richards Bay, on the north coast of Natal, work is proceeding on the construction of a multi-million dollar new port and city with more than 1 200 hectares set aside for general industrial development. The port area will be able to handle ships of up to 250 000 tons. A large petrochemical complex is also being constructed. An aluminium smelter is already in operation.

Photo: R. G. Greaves of Zululand Studios

The Hendrik Verwoerd dam, situated on the upper Orange River is part of the giant Orange River development project, one of the largest water supply schemes undertaken in Africa. On completion it will provide 320 megawats of hydro-electric power, and will irrigate 294 000 ha. of previously barren land in the southern and central Cape and Free State provinces.

Photo: S.A. Panorama

TRAINING & RESEARCH

A laboratory assistant testing equipment in the South African Bureau of Standards' Department of Chemical Technology. The SABS was established in 1945 as an autonomous body to promote standardization in industry and commerce, to prepare specifications and codes of practice with quality as criteria, and to provide facilities for the examination and testing of raw materials and commodities. It has a staff of more than 1 000 scientists, technicians and administrative personnel.

Photo: S.A. Panorama

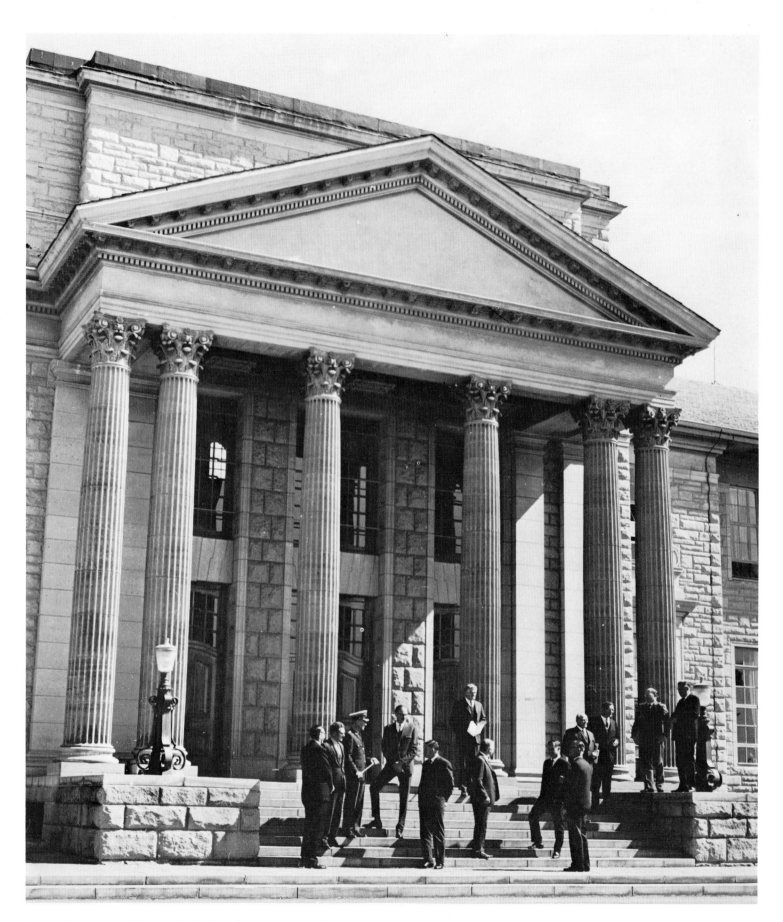

The administrative building of the Railway College, Esselen Park, near Kempton Park, Transvaal. The college was established in 1943 to help meet the demand for skilled manpower in the country's sprawling transport services. The Railways Department alone employs more than 230 000 workers. Italian prisoners of war helped to construct the building and their sophisticated workmanship can clearly be seen in its classical lines.

Photo: S.A. Panorama

Two aerial views of the headquarters of the Council
for Scientific and Industrial Research, Pretoria. It
is the largest research organisation in South Africa
and has a scientific staff of 600, supported by 1 000
technicians and administrative officials. It provides
the State, industry and community with the benefits
of modern research.

Photo: CSIR

A night view of the main building of the University of South Africa in Pretoria, which claims a student enrolment of more than 25 000. There are 11 universities for Whites in the Republic, with a combined student enrolment of more than 85 000.

Photo: S.A. Panorama

Groote Schuur Hospital, Cape Town, site of the world's first heart transplant performed by Professor Chris Barnard in December, 1967. The hospital also serves as a training centre for the University of Cape Town's medical students. Medical training in the Republic compares favourably with that offered in the world's top industrial countries. There are five medical schools (one of which, at Natal University, is exclusively for Blacks and Indians) with a combined enrolment of more than 3 000 students.

Photo: Protea Colour – Cape Town

A scientist of the Department of Agricultural Technical Services engaged in research work on fodder plants. Agricultural research costs nearly R1 million a year. The veterinary research establishment at Onderstepoort, near Pretoria, is the largest and most advanced in Africa.

Photo: S.A. Panorama

Trainee technicians receive instruction at the Post Office College at Olifantsfontein, near Jan Smuts Airport. The subject is modern micro-wave technology.

Photo: S.A. Panorama

The Pretoria-based Council of Scientific and Industrial Research (CSIR) utilises several windtunnels in its aero-dynamics research projects. The largest has an interior diameter of three metres and a maximum air speed of more than four times the speed of sound. Pictured are scientists facing a windtunnel of 2 m x 1,5 m. The CSIR was established in 1945. It comprises 16 research institutes and employs more than 700 scientists.

Photo: CSIR

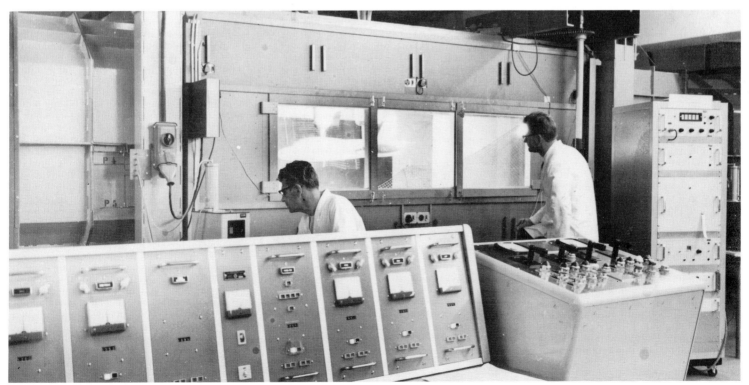

In-job training for Blacks is offered both in the public and private sector. Skilled Black workers in the Republic are the best paid in Africa. Pictured above are Black employees of S.A. Breweries participating in one of the company's training programmes. Thousands of Blacks in the public sector receive some form of in-job training, notably in the Post Office and Railway Departments.

The picture below shows Black students undergoing practical training in a laboratory of the University of the North at Turfloop, Northern Transvaal.

Photos: S.A. Panorama

Apart from in-service training, prospective Black scientists and technicians are trained at the University of South Africa (vacation schools) and three universities that cater for them. Pictured are two senior chemistry students working in a laboratory of the University of South Africa, Pretoria.

Photo: S.A. Panorama

Indian students in the chemistry laboratory of the
University of Durban-Westville.

Photo: Raymond Otte

Coloured wine-stewards are taught the finer points
of their trade at the S.A. Hotel Board's training
centre in Cape Town.

Photo: Eckley Dykman

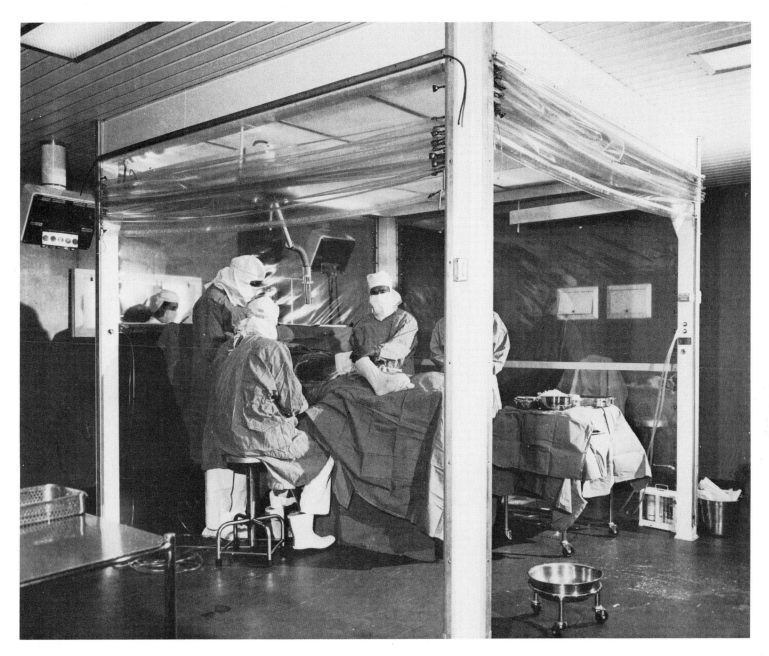

This clean operating enclosure was introduced as a permanent facility of the Orthopaedic Department of the H. F. Verwoerd Hospital in Pretoria. It involves the adaptation of industrial clean booths and so-called 'absolute' filters and reduces to a minimum the possibility of wound contamination by airborne bacteria during surgical operations. The Verwoerd Hospital serves as a training centre for medical students in the University of Pretoria's medical faculty.

Photo: CSIR

Wines are tested in the laboratory of the Oenological
Viticultural Research Institute at Groot Constantia, near Cape
Town, to determine whether they meet legal requirements.
On the experimental farm, Nietvoorbij, outside Stellenbosch,
the Institute carries out research into all aspects of viticulture
and wine production.

Photo: Samuel Kock

S.A. Bureau of Standards officials and installation engineers are dwarfed by this 15-ton 800 000 V testing transformer commissioned by the SABS. The transformer stands 11 metres high and will be used, inter alia, to test high voltage equipment and powerlines. The testing equipment of the Bureau, worth close on R5 million, is spread over 55 main laboratories. It has already prepared about 1 300 standard specifications, 1 000 private specifications, approximately 150 codes of practice and 700 test methods.

Photo: SABS

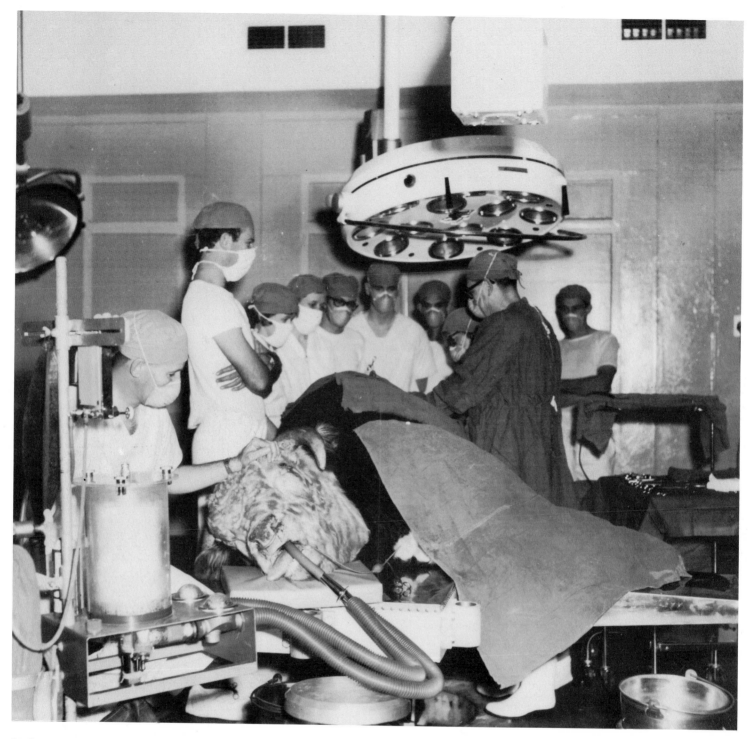

Students at the Ondersepoort Veterinary Research Institute attend an operation on a prize bull. The Institute is world famous for its research attracting scientists from the USA to Pakistan. In one year it produces more than 150 million doses of prophylactic vaccines for 35 different diseases. Vaccines are sent to many African states to aid in combatting viral diseases and bacterial infections.

Photo: University of Pretoria

The National Nuclear Research Centre at Pelindaba near Pretoria. Owing to the country's extensive reserves of low-cost uranium, the Atomic Energy Board is pursuing a comprehensive programme of applied nuclear research. The development of a new method for enriching uranium was announced in 1970 and the Uranium Enrichment Corporation (UCOR) was established in 1971 to further the development of this process. The Pelindaba centre offers a wide selection of research opportunities for specialists in the natural sciences.

Photo: Colin Jansen and Atomic Energy Board

An aerial view of the University of Durban-Westville. With more than 2 300 students, this is the only fully-fledged Indian university outside India. More than a quarter of the staff are Indians. Approximately 1 700 Indians are enrolled for correspondence courses at the University of South Africa and some 900 attend other South African residential Universities. Apart from the university, there are close on 400 Indian schools and two Indian colleges of education.

Photo: Raymond Otte

After basic university study in the engineering and natural sciences, many men and women move on to more advanced practical training and research in the laboratories that serve a wide variety of industrial and service establishments in both the private and public sector. Pictured is part of a chemical treatment process in the research laboratory of a minerals processing pilot plant at Germiston, in the Transvaal.

Photo: Johannesburg Consolidated Investment Co.

The central campus of the University of Pretoria. The Republic's 16 universities play a vital role in the training of highly skilled manpower, especially in the rapidly growing mining and manufacturing industries. A steadily growing supply of scientific manpower is a major factor in South Africa's leading economic position in the African continent, with the Republic already accounting for 40 per cent of the continent's entire industrial production.

Photo: University of Pretoria

126

Peaches being dried in the sun.
The Republic is the continent's top producer
and exporter of deciduous fruit.

Photo: Chris Jansen

The semi-arid region of the lower Orange River is well-known for its rich agricultural potential, particularly lucern, sultana grapes and dates. Pictured is a cluster of date palms at the Roman Catholic Mission at Pella. Some 11 metric tons of dates are marketed annually in South Africa.

Photo: S.A. Panorama

The Hex River Valley in the Western Cape is not only one of the greatest scenic attractions but also is one of the most fertile agricultural areas in the country. It is especially renowned for its splendid mosaic of vineyards and top quality grapes produced for the Republic's wine industry. South African wines and spirits have won many gold medals at international exhibitions.

Photo: Terence McNally

A Cape wine farm, with grapes ripening. The genesis
of the country's wine industry dates back to the
establishment of the Cape as a victualling station for
the Dutch East Indian Company in 1652. South
African white and red wines compare favourably
with those produced in the traditional wine producing
countries such as France and Germany.

Photo: Da Gama

Maize is one of the Republic's major field crops with
a gross value of close on R170 million.

Photo: Maize Board

The fruit-receiving area at the orange-juice plant at
Letaba, Northern Transvaal. A substantial part of the
country's orange crop is converted into fruit juice.

Photo: S.A. Panorama

Millions of sun-ripened oranges are harvested every season. A Major portion of the crop is exported.

Photo: Da Gama

A typical harvest scene on an apple farm in the Western Cape. A steadily growing portion of the country's apple production is processed into fruit juice.

Photo: Da Gama

A field of tobacco. Many parts of the country are ideally suited for this type of farming.

Photo: S.A. Panorama

Pineapples are produced in large quantities in the semi-tropical areas of Natal, the Southern Cape and the Eastern Transvaal Lowveld.

Photo: S.A. Panorama

South Africa ranks seventh among the 57 sugar producing countries of the world. Pictured is sugar cane ready to be processed into sugar.

Photos: S.A. Panorama

Completed
water from

Photo: Oran

More than 11 million hectares are already under
some 90 per cent of local demand. Exotic trees s
the private sector to augment indigenous source

Photo: S.A. Panorama

A Sugar
pictured
Many ex
finest in

Photo: S.

Mechanisation plays an increasingly impor
plantation pine, known as ''SA Pine''. This
favourably with types of pine traditionally in
approximately 3,25 million cubic metres of

Photo: Department of Forestry

Moorreesburg in the South-Western Cape, one of the country's main wheat growing districts. This area,
popularly known as the Swartland, was opened up for crop farming shortly after the establishment of the
Cape as a refreshment post for the Dutch in 1652. In 1968/1969 the Republic became self-supporting when the
total production of 1,2 million metric tons exceeded the demand by some 3 100 metric tons. Since then, wheat
production has consistently expanded. The summer rainfall regions of the Orange Free State and Transvaal
have become the major producers. Current production averages 1,6 million metric tons annually as against
an annual consumption of about 1,4 million metric tons.

Photo: Samuel Kock

146

Workers on a honey farm preparing hives for the new season. Honey farming dates back to the coming of the first pioneer farmers to the Cape three centuries ago.

Photo: Raymond Otte

147

An Afrikander bull. The Afrikander breed of cattle originated in South Africa and is world famous for the quality of its meat and its resistance to drought and disease.

Photo: SATOUR

Ostriches in a field of lucern – an everyday scene around Oudtshoorn in the South-Western Cape. About a century ago ostrich feather farming earned more money than any other agricultural industry in South Africa. After the First World War the industry declined rapidly and it began te re-establish itself only fairly recently when fashion once again began to look favourably upon the ostrich feather.

Photo: S.A. Panorama

The Roodeplaat Dam in the Pienaar's River, Transvaal.

Photo: S.A.R. Publicity and Travel Department

TOURISM

The splendid white coastline of the Cape South Coast, near Plettenberg Bay.

Photo : SATOUR

A striking aerial view of the Cape Peninsula, described by Sir Francis Drake as the 'fairest Cape' in the world. Fronting Table Mountain are Cape Town (founded in 1652) and Table Bay.

The population of Cape Town and its satellite towns numbers more than a million. The distinctive profile of Table Mountain is often the first glimpse that many tourists travelling by sea get of South Africa. More than half a million tourists visit the country annually.

Photo: Terence McNally

An approaching thunder storm near Golden Gate in the eastern Orange Free State looms large over the popular rest camp of the National Parks Board.

Photo: National Parks Board

A Southern Suns Hotel at Sea Point, Cape Peninsula, stands in splendour against the backdrop of Lion's Head. The country is serviced by more than 1500 licensed hotels ranging from small country inns to luxurious establishments.

Photo: S.A. Panorama

154

Members of an elephant clan somnolent in the midday heat of the Kruger National Park. Within the Republic's borders there are close on 200 public game and nature sanctuaries.

Photo: SATOUR

A popular view from Chapman's Peak across the blue water of Hout Bay, Cape Peninsula. Hout Bay, headquarters of the Peninsula's lobster fleet, is famous for its picturesque fishing harbour.

The 'Twelve Apostles', a range of distinctive peaks, towering over the white beaches of Clifton and Camps Bay, Cape Peninsula. The 80 kilometre seaboard route from Cape Town to Cape Point is known as the Marine Drive, reportedly one of the most picturesque seaboard routes in the world.

Photos: SATOUR

A restful country scene in the Little Karoo, near Oudtshoorn, Cape.

Photo: SATOUR

Table Bay, with Cape Town and Table Mountain in the background.
Below is a typical holiday resort on the Cape South Coast.

Photos : SATOUR

The lush and tranquil beauty of the Eastern Orange Free State countryside, near Golden Gate. Below is a section of the Blyde River Canyon, North-Eastern Transvaal. This part of the Republic, popular with tourists, has now become known as the Panorama route.

Photos: SATOUR

The restfulness and scenic splendours of the Tsitsikama coast on the Cape Garden Route. The top picture shows the Tsitsikama rest camp of the National Parks Board. Caravan camping is a major attraction on this picturesque route.

Photos: National Parks Board

The 'amphitheatre' in the Drakensberg range, Natal.

Photo: SATOUR

Spring daisies in the Western Cape. These great carpets of wild flowers are one of the country's major tourist attractions. With more than 16 000 species, South Africa has perhaps the richest flora in the world. Some 2 000 species of daisies grace the South African veld.

Photo: SATOUR

The Dutch Reformed Church at George, Cape South Coast, is typical of many to be found in the Western Cape.

Photo: Francois le Roux

A peaceful caravan park and camping site on the banks of the Touw River at the Wilderness, near George, the Cape South Coast.

Photo: Francois le Roux

Two aerial glimpses of Pretoria, the Republic's administrative capital. Pictured above are the city centre and the main streets running from east to west. Below are parts of the city's eastern and northern suburbs. Situated in the centre are the Union Buildings where the Ministers of several government departments have their offices.

Photos: Pretoria City Council, Publicity Division

The famous seaside resort of Muizenberg, Cape Peninsula, is unrivalled for its white beaches and glorious surf. Beyond the high-rise block of flats is the Hottentots Holland mountain range, and the famous 'white horses' of False Bay.

Photo: J. L. Moss

Plettenberg Bay, widely believed in tourist circles to be one of the finest holiday spots in the world. The popular Beacon Island Hotel in the foreground is situated on a small peninsula, offering the visitor a splendid mosaic of scenic vistas in every direction.

Photo: Protea Colour

A breadfruit tree – one of the oldest trees in the world – on the summit of a ridge at Houghton Johannesburg, keeps an eye on one of the world's youngest cities. With a population of more than 1,2 million, Johannesburg is South Africa's largest city and ranks third on the continent.

Photo: John Pitts

The majestic Strijdom Tower, overlooking a wide expanse of Johannesburg and the Witwatersrand, is the tallest man-made structure on the African continent. High as an 88-storey building, it is used for Post Office telecommunication purposes and for the micro-wave telephone system.

Photo: SATOUR

One of South Africa's Boeing 747's flying over Durban, Africa's premier port harbour. Owing to its mild winters, Durban is one of the most popular all-round tourist centres in South Africa.

Photo: SATOUR

Pictured above is an aerial view of Durban's beachfront, viewed from the north. Below is the same stretch of beach viewed from the south and photographed at night. Durban, caressed by the warm Mocambique current, is the country's most popular holiday resort during the winter. It has a population of more than half a million.

Photos: SATOUR

Another view of Durban, South Africa's premier seaport and holiday resort.

Photo: SATOUR

Clifton, Cape Peninsula. Local residents claim that the four beaches of this prestigeous Cape Town suburb have the whitest and finest sand on the country's coastline. The beaches are divided by rocky outcrops on which hundreds of bungalows cling picturesquely to the steep flank of Lion's Head.

Photo: SATOUR

Shingwedzi, one of 14 rest camps in the Kruger National Park. The Kruger Park covers an area the size of Wales or the State of Massachussetts, and is one of the best known game sanctuaries in the world. The 10 parks controlled by the National Parks Board attract more than 600 000 visitors each year.

Photo: National Parks Board

Black mineworkers performing traditional dances are a top drawcard for tourists visiting the major mine producing areas of the Republic. The bands are organised along ethnic lines with a strong competitive spirit pervading the dance sessions.

Photo : Electricity Supply Commission

A Xhosa boy enjoying the wild beauty of Cove Rock on the Transkei coast. The Transkei government is anxious to make the tourism industry one of its chief sources of economic growth.

Photo: Aubrey Elliot – The Magic World of the Xhosa

A pipe-smoking Xhosa woman in tribal dress. This scene is typical of the Black homelands where traditional life-styles are still very much in evidence. An increasing number of tourists are now visiting the ethnic homelands to see the large variety of tribal traditions in an equal diversity of natural settings.

Photo: Aubrey Elliott – The Magic World of the Xhosa

174

The unique Ndebele tribes of the Transvaal are greatly admired for their architecture and design. The houses of their villages are built on the simplest rectangular plans and designs adhere closely to the traditional geometrical motifs. Extensive use is made of natural earth colours incorporating bright commercial pigments on the entrance walls.

Above is a proud matron standing in the doorway of her spotless home.

A scene strangely reminiscent of an archaic temple with an ancient priestess at the entrance.

Photos: Esme Berman

A panoramic view from the top of the 'Amphitheatre' revealing some of the many beautiful peaks in the Drakensberg range. The 'Dragon Mountains' were given their name because of an imaginary resemblance to the rough profile of a dragon.

Photo: SATOUR

Table Bay, with an interesting silhouette of Table Mountain in the background. The 'vygie' blooms are typical of the Western Cape Coast. The mile upon mile phalanxes of froth-crested waves rolling on to the seemingly endless white beach of Blouberg Strand never fail to enthrall the visitor.

Photo: SATOUR

PROFILE FOR INVESTORS

Resumé

The Republic of South Africa is the politically most stable and economically most advanced country on the continent – in fact, the only country in Africa classified by the International Monetary Fund and the International Bank as having advanced beyond the stage of a "developing" economy.

According to the latest estimates (30 June 1972), South Africa had a population of almost 23 million, i.e. the fourth largest in Africa, and if present rates of growth and immigration should continue the total population will reach 50 million shortly after the year 2000 and 80 million by the year 2020.

Measured in terms of its gross domestic product, i.e. the total production of goods and services within its borders, the South African economy is about seven times the "size" of any other African country south of the Sahara and its per capita national income is about five times the average for the rest of Africa.

The stake of other industrial countries in this development has been considerable and will no doubt remain large. For although South Africa has a high rate of saving by international standards, it has always welcomed foreign participation in its economic development, not only for the sake of the funds as such but also for the sake of the skilled manpower, technical know-how, marketing expertise and the contacts abroad which usually go with foreign investment. The foreign investor has found South Africa a safe and profitable haven for his capital, as appears from the large amounts of capital which have in fact been flowing into this country over many decades.

In other respects too, the rest of the developed world has a significant interest in the South African economy. This applies to foreign trade, for instance, for South Africa has a very "open" economy, with exports and imports each amounting to about 20 per cent of the gross domestic product. In spite of a widening range of manufactured exports South Africa still mainly supplies primary products to the Western industrial countries and to Japan, and imports mainly manufactured capital and intermediate goods from these countries.

Notwithstanding certain natural disadvantages, South Africa has built up a well developed infrastructure – including the most extensive rail, road and air traffic networks as well as the highest power generating capacity in Southern Africa – to serve as the foundation for the rapidly developing superstructure of agricultural, mining, manufacturing and service activities.

One factor which, at times of exceptionally rapid economic growth in South Africa, tends to exercise a restrictive effect after a certain point is the relative scarcity of highly trained manpower and entrepreneurship in contrast to a relative abundance of untrained manpower. This problem is, however, receiving the serious attention of the authorities and millions of rands are being spent annually to train and re-orient the Black population in particular to adjust themselves to the higher demands of an industrial society.

This is a very necessary development because the South African economy, which is still thought by many people abroad to be largely an agricultural and mining economy, is in fact rapidly becoming diversified and industrialised. This appears clearly from the fact that the contribution of manufacturing industry to the gross domestic product has increased from only about 7 per cent in the twenties to about 23 per cent at present, and this structural shift is still continuing and gathering speed.

What is true, however, is that the rise in the relative importance of secondary industry has to a large extent been made possible by the abundance and variety of locally available raw materials supplied by the mining and agricultural industries, which also earn much of the foreign exchange required to stock and equip the burgeoning manufacturing sector. Concurrently with these developments the country's banking and other financial institutions have also reached a high degree of diversification and sophistication and have proved themselves perfectly capable of providing all the necessary services to commerce and industry.

Finally, it is a fact that South Africa's rapid economic development has in no small way been attributable to the sympathetic approach and active stimulation of successive governments, which have seen it as their task, firstly, to create the necessary conditions for the unfettered and secure development of the free enterprise system and, secondly, to take the initiative in development projects essential to a particular stage of economic growth when private enterprise for some reason or other did not respond to the challenge. The authorities have also been extremely sympathetic to the needs of other territories in Southern Africa because they regard South Africa's well-being as inextricably bound up with that of the rest of Africa.

Infrastructure

In spite of certain natural disadvantages, such as an almost complete lack of navigable rivers and a large land area in relation to its total population, with consequent long distances between the metropolitan centres, the Republic of South Africa has one of the best developed, and most rapidly developing, infrastructures of any country on the continent. Without this solid foundation the extensive superstructure of agricultural, mining, manufacturing and service activities could not have been built up and maintained.

As regards transport, the country is well equipped with an efficient network of railways, all-weather roads and airways as well as several large harbours. This is clearly illustrated by a few comparative figures. Thus, South Africa has more than 22 000 kilometers of railways, which is more than six times the length of railways in any other area in Southern Africa. Angola, with a land area comparable to that of South Africa, has only about 3 600 kilometers of railways, and Zambia, with its relatively strong copper-based economy, a little more than 1 000 kilometers.

Similarly, South Africa has about 35 000 kilometers of tarred roads, as compared with about 7 000 kilometers in the case of Rhodesia, 4 600 in the case of Angola and 2 500 in Zambia, to mention only a few of the larger territories in Southern Africa.

As regards the relative size of the vehicle "population", South Africa has about 1 car to every 10 persons, whereas the comparative figures (number of persons per car) for some other Southern African territories are: South West Africa 12,5, Rhodesia 30,1, Zambia 43,3, Botswana 98,8 and Malawi 243,3.

Although South Africa has no natural harbours the country nevertheless has five modern and well-equipped man-made harbours, namely Table Bay (Cape Town), Algoa Bay (Port Elizabeth), Buffalo Harbour (East London) and Durban, as well as Walvis Bay in South West Africa. Important harbour development is also taking place at Saldanha Bay on the west coast and Richards Bay on the east coast.

Of all the various forms of transport in South Africa, air transport has shown the most rapid growth in recent years. Thus the total number of passengers carried on internal and overseas services have increased more than tenfold from 1951 to 1972, i.e. from 167 866 to 1 844 286. Mail and freight traffic by air increased even more spectacularly over the same period.

Turning now to the communications media, South Africa is also well-equipped to provide the necessary services to the rapidly growing business community. Thus, according to the latest available statistics, the country has 69 telephones and 144 radio receivers per 1 000 inhabitants and about 40 copies of daily newspapers are distributed per 1 000 inhabitants. These figures are among the highest on the continent and they are increasing at a progressive rate in conjunction with the rising standards of living of the Black population in particular.

Because it is so basic to industrial development especially, the increase in power generated in a country is frequently taken as a yardstick of its growth. In the case of South Africa the number of units generated has grown at an average annual rate of 8,1 per cent over the past decade (1962-72). Per capita private consumption expenditure for electricity increased at an average annual rate of 5,6 per cent over the same period. Measured against these yardsticks South Africa is undoubtedly one of the most rapidly developing countries in Africa, and these rates also compare favourably with those of many developed countries.

By far the larger part of South Africa's economic infrastructure (railways, harbours, airways, road construction, postal, telephone, telegraph and radio services as well as the generation of power) is supplied and controlled by the public sector, mostly in the form of public enterprises operated on business principles. This makes for efficiency in the provision of these services, while at the same time ensuring that even the most remote and thinly populated parts of the country will be supplied with the necessary services to stimulate their development.

Population and National Income

At the date of the last population census (1970) the Republic of South Africa had a total population of 21 448 169. By 30 June 1972 the population had increased to 22 987 000, according to the latest mid-year estimate by the South African Department of Statistics. Of the latter figure the various Black nations formed the largest single group, namely 16 217 000 (70,5 per cent), while the Whites numbered 3 958 000 (17,2 per cent), Coloureds, i.e. persons of mixed descent, 2 144 000 (9,3 per cent) and Asians 668 000 (2,9 per cent). This makes South Africa the country with the fourth largest population in Africa, and although in terms of Government policy the various Black nations in the present Republic of South Africa are to form their own independent states in the foreseeable future, it is envisaged that they will remain part of a South African common market so that the market will not be fragmented.

The rate of growth of the South African population is fairly high as compared with most Western countries. For the decade 1960-70 the average annual rate of growth for the total population was 2,7 per cent. This takes into account the effect of immigration, without which the rate of growth would have been somewhat lower (2,5 per cent). If the present rates of growth and immigration should continue the country's total population will be about 47 million by the year 2 000 and close on 80 million in 50 years' time, i.e. by the year 2020.

Measured in terms of its gross domestic product, i.e. the total production of goods and services within its borders, the South African economy is more or less comparable in "size" to that of Denmark and is approximately half the "size" of the Australian Dutch or Swedish economies but about seven times the "size" of any other economy in Africa south of the Sahara.

The average annual rate of growth of the South African gross domestic product at constant prices during the decade of the sixties was 6,1 per cent, which was among the highest in the world and also among the highest on the African continent. In the very recent past this rate has dropped somewhat but this was due to short-term factors and at the present stage it is rising again.

The per capita national income in South Africa amounted to $794 in 1972. Although this was about five times the average figure for the rest of Africa it was still rather low by comparison with other Western countries. The reason for this is that, as in the rest of Africa, a substantial number of the country's Black population still practice subsistence agriculture, with a very low per capita income. This situation is changing rapidly, however, as growing numbers of the Black population are drawn into the modern sector of the economy, where incomes compare favourably with those in the industrialised countries of the world.

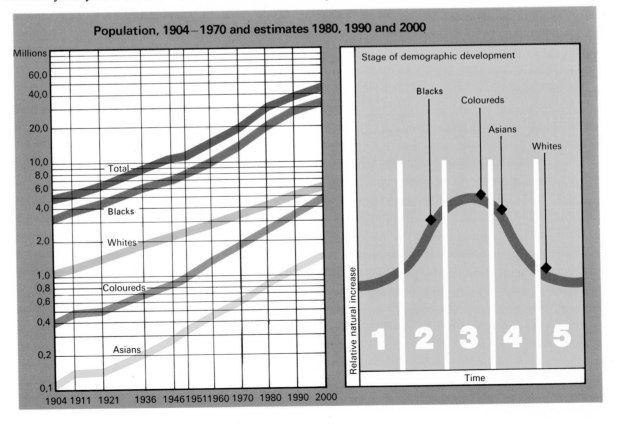

Banking and Financial Institutions

Although the banking and financial system in South Africa is relatively young as compared with those in Western Europe, it is already widely diversified in accordance with the needs of the economy, and the quality of the services rendered by the various types of credit institutions compares favourably with those anywhere in the world.

At the top of the banking and financial pyramid in South Africa there is the South African Reserve Bank which, together with the other "monetary authority", the Department of Finance, is responsible for the financial stability and adaptability of the economy. The Reserve Bank, which was established in 1920 and has its head office in Pretoria, keeps a watchful eye on the whole credit structure of the country and is also responsible for the implementation of the exchange control regulations and the sale of South Africa's gold production. The Bank has, over the years, won itself an enviable reputation for level-headed conservatism combined with a willingness to deviate from old norms if this is what the country's interests demand.

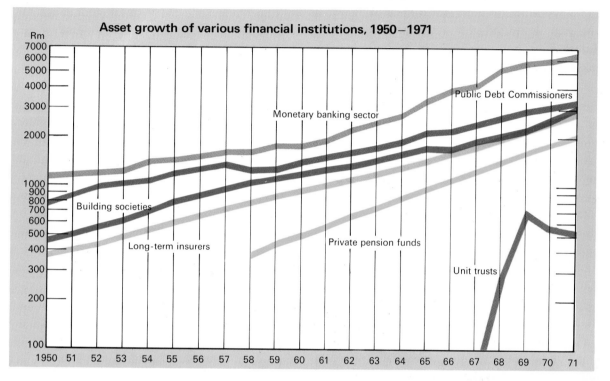

Asset growth of various financial institutions, 1950–1971

Closely allied to the Reserve Bank is the National Finance Corporation of South Africa which was established by means of legislation in 1949 as a first step in the development of an active money market in South Africa. Since then the money market has attained a high degree of sophistication and the National Finance Corporation has therefore fulfilled its function of stimulating this development. The Corporation still accepts demand and time deposits from the public and invests these funds in the securities of public and semi-public bodies.

The base of the banking pyramid in South Africa is the commercial banks. There are 9 registered commercial banks in South Africa at present with an extensive network of almost 3 000 branches and agencies serving even the most far-off parts of the country. Commercial banks except deposits and make advances to the general public and the business community and also administer cheque accounts for their clients. They are authorised dealers in foreign exchange and consequently they all have foreign exchange accounts overseas, which enable them to play an active part in the financing of external trade. The total assets of the commercial banks have increased from $2 400 million in December 1963 to $7 500 million in September 1973.

Merchant banks first appeared on the South African scene about 17 years ago and were based on the same principles as the merchant banks in the "City" of London. At present there are 9 merchant banks in South Africa which supply short-term credit to finance the movement of goods as well as the import and export of merchandise.

The growing sophistication of the money market has also in due course led to the establishment of 3 discount houses by the merchant banks in co-operation with certain other interests. The discount houses receive deposits from the merchant banks, commercial banks, building societies, mining houses, etc. and use these funds mainly to discount the acceptances of merchant banks.

In the general banking sphere there are three further types of institutions active in the South African economy, namely "general" banks, of which there are 19 and which provide long-term loans for a wide variety of purposes; 2 hire-purchase banks, which provide credit for the purchase of durable consumer goods; and 8 savings banks, which provide advances to individuals against the security of fixed property or sureties.

Other types of financial institutions of a more specialised nature include a number of building societies, which provide loans for residential building purposes; the Industrial Development Corporation of South Africa, which was established by law in 1940 to encourage industrial development, *inter alia* through

181

the provision of medium and long-term finance; the Land and Agricultural Bank, which provides credit to the farming community; the Bantu, Xhosa and Coloured Development Corporations, which promote the development of industrial and commercial enterprises among the various Non-White population groups; the Johannesburg Stock Exchange; and a host of other financial institutions, such as mutual funds, pension funds, insurance firms, shipping, leasing and factoring companies, governmental savings facilities, etc.

It must be clear, however, that South Africa's banking and financial structure is highly developed and diversified and does a very good job of pumping the life-blood of business, namely finance, along the arteries of commerce and industry.

Foreign Investment

With a young, dynamically developing economy and a rapidly growing population to be provided with adequate employment opportunities, South Africa needs to maintain a high rate of investment. South Africa's savings rate, at some 25 per cent of its gross national product, is high by international standards. Although this means that by far the largest part of the required investment each year – normally well over 90 per cent – is financed from the country's own savings, South Africa has always welcomed foreign investment on account of the undoubted advantages it can impart to the economy, in particular in the form of the skilled personnel, technical know-how, and marketing expertise that usually go with foreign investment.

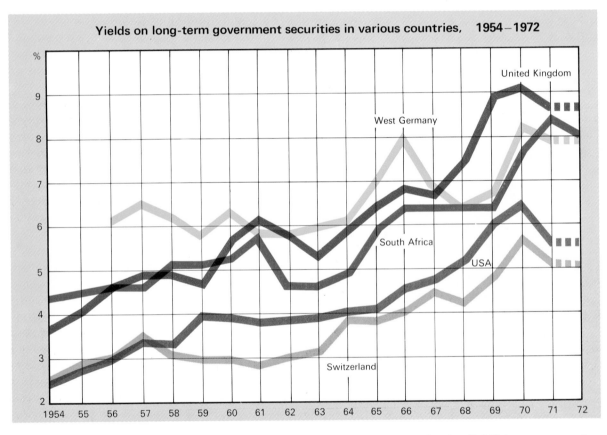

Yields on long-term government securities in various countries, 1954–1972

While South Africa has, therefore, actively encouraged foreign investment and studiously avoided actions which could endanger the interests of foreign investors, foreign investors in their turn have for long considered South Africa as a safe and rewarding country to which they may commit their funds. During the past decade the average annual yield on all foreign investment in South Africa has fluctuated between just below 10 per cent and over 12 per cent. If it is considered that this figure includes the payments on fixed interest-bearing loans by the private and public sectors, it is obvious that the yield on direct investments must be considerably higher.

It is no wonder, then, that South Africa has for several years experienced a steady net inflow of foreign capital, amounting to an average of over $700 million per annum from 1967 to 1972. Still, the country's foreign debt position has remained sound, as witness the fact that foreign liabilities as a percentage of the gross domestic product amounted to only 45 per cent on average during the same period. The confidence of foreign investors in the stability of the South African economy, and their satisfaction with the results of their investments in the country, is perhaps best attested to by the fact that over these five years, only two-thirds of the earnings on foreign investment in South Africa were actually taken out of the country, the rest having been re-invested in South Africa.

While in other African countries governments have taken to nationalisation of foreign-controlled enterprises, and even in some of the developed western countries foreign investors have of late been subjected to various restrictions, the South African government has repeatedly assured foreign investors that they are welcome to increase their stake in the South African economy.

Rather than the taking over of existing foreign investments by South African interests, the government prefers to see significant South African participation from the outset in new ventures undertaken by foreign investors in South Africa. In this way, it is felt, the South African participants do not only share in the eventual successes of such ventures, but in the initial risks as well.

External Trade

With the annual value of its exports and imports each amounting to some 20 per cent of the gross domestic product, South Africa is obviously a country with an established interest in international trade. Although the pattern of its trading relations with other countries used to be influenced significantly by its former membership of the British Commonwealth, South Africa was also one of the founding signatories of the General Agreement on Tariffs and Trade in 1947. Since that time, the country's foreign trade has been considerably diversified both in respect of the kinds of goods traded and the countries with which trading relations are maintained.

Whereas the contribution of gold to South Africa's foreign earnings on current account amounted to around 40 per cent in the years just after World War II, and its value then approached that of the country's exports of all other merchandise, the position has since then changed quite considerably. By 1972, before the sharp rise in its market price, gold contributed only 28 per cent of foreign earnings on current account, and the value of the net gold output in that year was $1 620 million, i.e. only slightly more than half the $3 000 million worth of other merchandise exports.

Agricultural produce, in particular wool, deciduous fruits, and in some years maize, as well as diamonds and a variety of base minerals, are among the more important merchandise exports of South Africa. However, exports of a widening range of manufactured goods have increased considerably, including such items as processed foodstuffs, textiles, and chemicals. In addition to gold production and merchandise exports, foreign earnings from services increased from less than $140 million just after World War II to more than $1 000 million, or 18 per cent of total foreign earnings, in 1972.

On the import side, finished consumer goods have declined in importance in accordance with the substitution of imports by locally manufactured consumer goods, and in recent years capital goods and intermediate goods have made up the bulk of South Africa's merchandise imports, which amounted to $3 900 million in 1972. Foreign payments for services increased from around $280 million in the early post-war years to $1 820 million in 1972.

From the figures quoted above, it is evident that South Africa occupies a position of some significance in world trade. The direction of the country's trade flows has, moreover, changed quite considerably over the past decade. Whereas in the early 1960s some 30 per cent of South Africa's merchandise imports originated in the United Kingdom, this share had fallen to just over 20 per cent in 1972. Over the same period, the share provided by West Germany to South Africa's total merchandise imports rose from below 11 to around 15 per cent, and of Japan from 5 to 9,5 per cent, while the share of the United States declined marginally to just below 17 per cent, and those of the remaining European Community and Asian countries rose slightly. Similarly, the share of the United Kingdom and the United States in South Africa's merchandise exports declined from well over 50 to well below 40 per cent over the same period, while that of Japan in particular increased considerably.

If the net gold production is excluded from the foreign earnings on current account, it appears that South Africa has a negative trade balance with all the major world trading regions except Africa, in respect of which the favourable balance was $319 million in 1972. The negative trade balance with the European Community was $611 million in 1972, with all American countries $427 million, with Asia $199 million, and with Oceania $39 million. It follows that many countries, in most parts of the world, derive quite significant benefits from their trading relations with South Africa.

Natural Resources

Climatic conditions in South Africa differ widely between various regions, which enables the agricultural industry to produce a wide diversity of crops. There are vast, fairly arid areas suited mainly to sheep farming on an extensive basis, as well as large temperate and sub-tropical regions suitable for pastoral farming on a more intensive basis or for the growing of field crops. In addition, there is a winter-rainfall area with a mediterranean climate excellently suited to viticulture and fruit-growing. It is not surprising therefore that imported agricultural products form less than 2 per cent of the total value of South Africa's merchandise imports, the most important products imported being tea, rice, coffee, cocoa beans and unprocessed rubber.

On the whole, however, South Africa is not particularly well endowed with agricultural resources. As a result of various factors, including low and unpredictable rainfall with frequent droughts over large areas, poor soil conditions, etc., only about 15 per cent of the land mass is cultivatable and only about 1 per cent irrigable.

Determined efforts have been made over a long period both by the private sector and the authorities to mitigate the effects of these natural disadvantages by means of irrigation projects, such as the giant Orange River Project now under construction, State-supported soil conservation programmes, the large-scale application of fertilisers, and research into plant and animal diseases which has in many cases received international acclaim.

The Government is also actively engaged in an extensive programme aimed at introducing more modern and productive agricultural methods in the areas occupied by Black farmers where, until quite recently, farming has been practised mainly on a traditional subsistence basis. It is to be expected that this introduction of more modern techniques will in due course considerably enhance the country's agricultural production and the capacity of the land to sustain higher incomes.

As regards mineral resources, South Africa is richly endowed, judged by international standards, and it is frequently called "the treasure house of the world". Although South Africa constitutes only 0,8 per cent of the world's surface and its population only 0,5 per cent of the world population, it produces about three-quarters of the free world's gold. It is also the world's largest producer of diamonds by value and, since 1953, has been the biggest producer of platinum. South Africa produces more than 90 per cent of all coal mined in Africa and its coal reserves represent 80 per cent of the estimated reserves in Africa. South Africa also has large deposits, or ranks among the world's major producers of uranium, chromite, manganese, asbestos, antimony, corundum and vanadium. In addition, South Africa (and South West Africa, whose economy is to a large extent integrated with that of South Africa) possesses and exploits a wide variety of other minerals, some of them in large quantities. These include iron, copper, silver, nickel, tungsten, zinc, mica, tin, lead, titanium, phosphates, beryllium and zirconium, to mention only a few.

South Africa is one of the few countries in the world which have deposits of all the important minerals needed for the alloying of steel.

The most important minerals not found in mineable quantities in South Africa are bauxite, soda ash, sulphur, potassium, molybdenum and petroleum. As regards petroleum the South African Government has mounted an intensive exploration programme in search of mineable deposits of natural oil in South Africa or in its coastal waters, but so far without success. Fortunately for South Africa it is not as dependent on petroleum as a source of energy as is the case with most other industrial countries because of its large coal deposits (conservatively estimated at 75 000 000 000 tons) which serve as an alternative source of energy either directly or in the form of petrol produced from coal at Sasolburg.

As regards other natural resources, it may be mentioned that South Africa is among the top eight of the world's fish trading nations. Bordering on the Indian and Atlantic oceans and with a coast line of more than 3 000 kilometers South Africa has ample resources of marine foods and the exploitation of these resources has made rapid strides since the Second World War as a result of far-seeing State research and individual enterprise of a high order.

Owing to adverse climatic conditions South Africa, rich as it is in other resources, is poorly endowed with indigenous forest growth. The total forest area, indigenous and cultivated, amounts to some 3,5 million hectares or just under 1 per cent of the total land area, which is low as compared, for example, with the United States (commercial forest area 25 per cent) or Canada (27 per cent).

Mining

As indicated in the previous section, the Republic of South Africa is exceptionally well endowed with mineral resources and consequently the mining industry has played a major role in the economic development of the country. Over the five years 1967 to 1971 the average contribution of mining and quarrying to the gross domestic product was 11,1 per cent. This figure, however, is a very poor indication of the important part this industry has played, and is still playing, with regard to aspects such as the creation of employment opportunities, the earning of foreign exchange, the provision of markets, both for agriculture and for secondary industry, the production of low-priced raw materials for secondary industry in particular, the attraction of foreign investment capital, the shielding of the economy as a whole against extreme fluctuations in business activity, and many others.

Thus, over most of the period since the Second World War the mining industry has provided employment opportunities to 10-11 per cent of the total economically active population but to more than 15 per cent of the economically active Blacks in the country, including hundreds of thousands of "guest workers" from neighbouring countries where comparable employment opportunities are not available on the same scale.

From the point of view of exports and foreign exchange earnings the part played by the mining industry is even more impressive. No less than 39,2 per cent of South Africa's total exports (by value) in 1972 consisted of products of the mining and quarrying industry (including gold). Ever since the beginning of the century, the exports of the mining industry have to a large extent earned the necessary foreign exchange to finance the country's rapid industrialisation. With the recent rise in the price of gold and the strong world demand for many of the other minerals produced in South Africa there is little doubt that this situation will continue for some time in spite of the fact that exports of manufactured products have in recent years shown a tendency to increase more rapidly than mining and agricultural exports.

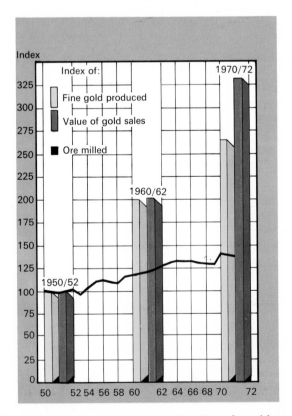

In other respects too the ready availability of a wide variety of mineral resources has been, and continue to be, very beneficial to the development of the South African economy, and the

184

process of industrialisation in particular. To mention only two examples of great significance for future development: The Republic has some of the largest and most easily mineable coal reserves in the world. Consequently the country produces the cheapest steam-generated electricity in the world, with obvious implications for industry, and at the same time this coal serves as the basis for a rapidly growing chemical industry producing a wide range of products which previously either had to be imported directly or to be manufactured from imported raw materials, such as crude petroleum.

The second example which may be mentioned is that South Africa has vast reserves of what is probably the most important industrial mineral of all, namely iron ore. In addition, the country also has reserves of practically all the metals required for the production of ferro-alloys, such as manganese, tin, nickel and vanadium. The production of various ferro-alloys is therefore a rapidly expanding industry in South Africa and in turn acts as a stimulus to many other sectors of secondary industry. It also forms part of a more general movement, which is strongly supported by the authorities, to ensure that South Africa's mineral riches will increasingly be exported in a beneficiated or processed form rather than in the crude form so as to ensure the maximum advantages for the country both in terms of foreign earnings and in terms of industrial development.

The following table shows the physical volume and the sales value of the most important minerals produced in 1972:

Mineral	Volume	Sales value (R1 000) (R1 = $1,4)
Gold (kg)	909 631	1 159 916
Silver (kg)	102 443	4 114
Iron ore (1 000 tons)	11 223	30 314
Chrome (1 000 tons)	1 483	12 809
Copper (1 000 tons)	162	116 591
Manganese ore (1 000 tons)	3 373	37 297
Diamonds (1 000 carats)	7 395	90 029
Coal (1 000 tons)	58 440	126 782
Lime and limestone (1 000 tons)	15 615	21 789
Asbestos (1 000 tons)	321	38 031
Phosphates (1 000 tons)	1 966	12 375
Salt (1 000 tons)	8 370	4 077
Fluorspar (1 000 tons)	211	4 446
Other minerals		283 773
Total		1 942 343 or $ 2,7 billion

Manufacturing Industry

Although in the eyes of the world the South African economy is largely associated with the gold mining industry, it has in actual fact come to be dominated to an ever-increasing extent by manufacturing industry. Whereas in the 1920s only some 7 per cent of the country's gross domestic product originated in secondary industry, this percentage has already reached 23 per cent and is still rising. Already some 15 per cent of the country's economically active population are employed in secondary industry, as against 9 per cent just after World War II.

The basis for South Africa's industrial development is to be found in the abundance and variety of locally available raw materials – in particular the availability of coal at very low pit-head cost, which has made possible the generation of electric power which can be sold at low rates, the ready availability of large supplies of trainable labour, the sophisticated financial and management experience which was built up as a byproduct of the mining developments, and the active encouragement of industrial development by successive governments.

Apart from an active policy of stimulating local industries by means of selective import tariffs, governments have encouraged industrial development by such means as the establishment of public corporations to undertake developments which were beyond the scope of private enterprise – as in the basic steel industry during the early 1930s and in the production of oil from coal in the 1950s; the establishment in 1940 of the Industrial Development Corporation to provide in the financing needs of viable industrial undertakings; and the establishment of the Council for Scientific and Industrial Research to provide in the research needs of the industrial sector.

In the earlier stages of South Africa's industrialisation, and even up to as recently as the 1950s, the development of industries was mainly aimed at the replacement of imported goods by locally manufactured goods, mainly consumer goods. This is reflected clearly in the composition of South Africa's industrial production at the time – thus, in 1916-17 73 per cent of the value of industrial output consisted of final consumer goods, and as late as 1946-47 this figure was still as high as 59 per cent. Since most consumer goods are today already being manufactured locally, however, the scope for further import replacement in this field is limited, and the attention of industrialists is shifting towards production for export and towards more local production of intermediate and capital goods, which already constituted around 50 per cent of the value of manufacturing output at the beginning of the 1970s.

Although South Africa has been able, through welcoming foreign investment in her industries over a wide range, to benefit considerably from imported industrial know-how, much has also been done locally in respect of research with industrial applications. Besides the Council for Scientific and Industrial Research, which has already been mentioned, and which *inter alia* provides facilities for the testing and further development of patentable inventions by private individuals, industrial research is also undertaken in a variety of other government-supported and private institutions. This has enabled South Africa, for example, to pioneer in the production of oil from coal by the South African Coal, Oil and Gas Corporation (whose large variety of byproducts has provided an important stimulus to the development of South Africa's chemical industries), while further research on alternative processes is in progress at the Fuel Research Institute in Pretoria. As a result of research done under the auspices of the Atomic Energy Board, South Africa's Uranium Enrichment Corporation is also at present in the process of implementing a revolutionary new technique of uranium enrichment. Apart from these more dramatic examples, many other instances can be quoted of research breakthroughs which have found useful industrial applications, illustrating that South Africa's manufacturing sector is well and truly able to stand on its own feet and make its expected contribution to the country's economic development.

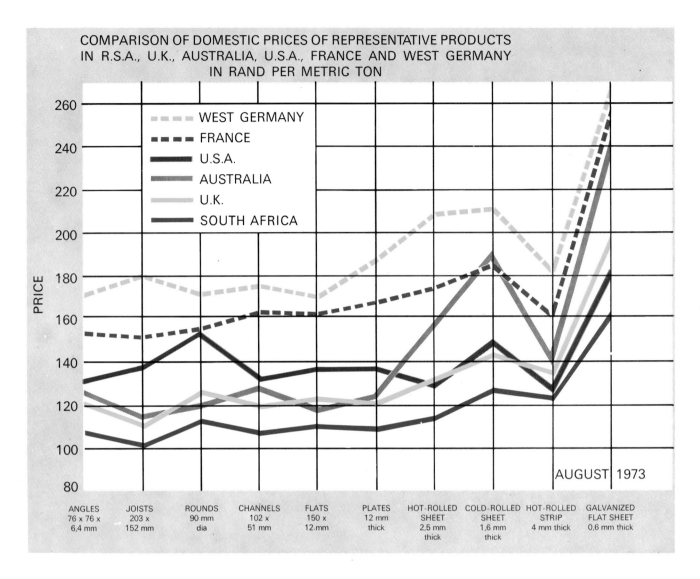

COMPARISON OF DOMESTIC PRICES OF REPRESENTATIVE PRODUCTS IN R.S.A., U.K., AUSTRALIA, U.S.A., FRANCE AND WEST GERMANY IN RAND PER METRIC TON

AUGUST 1973

Legend:
- WEST GERMANY
- FRANCE
- U.S.A.
- AUSTRALIA
- U.K.
- SOUTH AFRICA

X-axis categories:
ANGLES 76 x 76 x 6,4 mm | JOISTS 203 x 152 mm | ROUNDS 90 mm dia | CHANNELS 102 x 51 mm | FLATS 150 x 12 mm | PLATES 12 mm thick | HOT-ROLLED SHEET 2,5 mm thick | COLD-ROLLED SHEET 1,6 mm thick | HOT-ROLLED STRIP 4 mm thick | GALVANIZED FLAT SHEET 0,6 mm thick

Agriculture

Agriculture (including forestry and fishing) contributed 9,9 per cent to South Africa's gross domestic product in 1972, as compared with 11 per cent in the case of mining and more than 30 per cent in the case of secondary industry (including construction and electricity, gas and water). These relationships have undergone striking changes over the years, as is apparent from the fact that half a century earlier, in 1920, agriculture had contributed 22 per cent to the gross domestic product, as opposed to 19 per cent in the case of mining and only 10 per cent in the case of secondary industry. The physical volume of agricultural production has of course increased many times over during that period but its relative importance in the national product has declined owing to the fact that secondary industry has grown so much faster by comparison. This process is still continuing and in the Economic Development Programme for 1972-77 a rate of growth of 4,1 per cent was predicted for agricultural production over the period concerned, as against 6,4 per cent for manufacturing production and 5,75 per cent for the real gross domestic product as a whole.

The following table illustrates clearly the growth in the physical volume of agricultural production during the period since the Second World War:

Indices of physical volume of agricultural production
(1958/59 — 1960/61 = 100)

	Field crops	Horticultural products	Livestock products	Total
1947/48	68	53	70	67
1949/50	52	59	76	68
1954/55	81	78	90	84
1959/60	96	103	100	99
1964/65	116	134	110	116
1969/70	147	168	132	144
1970/71	175	177	129	155
1971/72	194	188	129	164
1972/73	130	186	130	139

Source: Department of Agricultural Economics and Marketing.

The major field crops produced, with the gross value (R1 = $1,4) for 1972-73 given in brackets, are maize (R167,0 m.), wheat (R123,1 m.), sugar cane (R92,3 m.), hay (R44,0 m.), ground nuts (R20,9 m.) and tobacco (R20,6 m.). The major horticultural crops are deciduous fruit (R77,2 m.), vegetables (R61,6 m.), viticulture (R53,1 m.), citrus fruit (R40,5 m.) and potatoes (R28,4 m). As regards animal products, the following are the most important: cattle and calves slaughtered (R240,9 m.), wool (R142,0 m.), sheep and goats slaughtered (R105,0 m.), fresh milk (R96,2 m.), dairy products (R62,6 m.), poultry slaughtered (R48,5 m.), eggs (R41,7 m.) and pigs slaughtered (R35,6 m.).

The importance of agriculture in the South African economy is not fully apparent from its contribution to the total output since it is also a major source of foreign exchange earnings and of employment opportunities. Thus processed and unprocessed agricultural exports (more or less in equal proportions) are normally responsible for about one-third of South Africa's total export earnings although there is a long-run tendency for this percentage to decline as the process of industrialisation proceeds and manufactured products therefore figure more prominently in the country's exports. The principal agricultural products exported are maize, sugar, wool, preserved fruit and jam, deciduous fruit and table grapes, citrus fruit, and hides and skins.

As regards employment opportunities, at the time of the last population census (1970) no less than 28 per cent (2 239 000) of South Africa's total economically active population of 7 986 000 were engaged in agriculture, forestry and fishing. In this respect, there are significant differences, however, between the various population groups. Thus only 6,6 per cent of the economically active Whites were engaged in agriculture in 1970 as against 36 per cent of the Blacks. These figures reflect the fact that the Blacks have not yet been drawn into the modern industrial economy to the same extent as the Whites. Unfortunately the productivity of many of the Black farmers is still very low owing to a variety of factors, but the authorities have been taking vigorous measures to improve this situation.

As pointed out earlier South Africa is among the world's major fish trading nations and the total catch (mainly pilchard, anchovy and true mackerel), exceeds those of many of the traditional fishing nations like Britain, West Germany and France. South Africa is now the world's second largest fish meal producer (after Peru) and is the largest producer of certain other fish products in the southern hemisphere.

It was pointed out earlier that climatic and other conditions in South Africa are not particularly suited to forestry. In spite of this South Africa has developed from a position of almost total reliance on imported timber to a point bordering on self-sufficiency in this regard.

Labour

South Africa's total labour force was estimated at 7 807 000 persons in 1971, and is expected to grow at an annual rate of 2,64 per cent up to the year 2 000. About a fifth of the labour force are Whites, with a level of training, in a wide variety of skills and professions, comparable to that of the labour forces of most developed western countries. Blacks (consisting of several different ethnic groups) comprise about 70 per cent of the total labour force, and although increasing numbers of these groups are receiving training of an ever more sophisticated nature, the majority are still employed either in subsistence agriculture or in semi-skilled and operative jobs in the modern sector of the economy. As regards their level of training, the Coloured and Asian population groups, who make up the rest of the labour force, occupy an intermediate position between the Whites and Blacks.

Labour legislation is based on the principle that Black workers receive preference in their homelands and White, Coloured, and Asian workers in the rest of the country. The main legislation affecting White, Coloured and Asian workers is embodied in the Industrial Conciliation Act, which provides for industrial councils in which representatives of workers and employers in the various sectors of the economy negotiate on wages and working conditions. The wages and working conditions of workers in the White areas for whom industrial councils do not exist, including Black workers, are determined in terms of the Wage Act by a statutory Wage Board, which undertakes periodic investigations in the respective industries. Communication between Black workers and their employers is effected through a system of in-plant works and liaison committees in terms of the Bantu Labour Regulations Amendment Act of 1973, and the interests of Black workers are also looked after by a Central Bantu Labour Board, which can make submissions to the Wage Board and to industrial councils on behalf of Black workers.

Both the Industrial Conciliation Act and the Wage Act enforce the principle of the rate for the job, so that the narrowing of the rather substantial income differences that still prevail between the different population groups, depend to a large extent on the rate at which Black, Coloured and Asian workers advance into higher-skilled jobs. In the White parts of the country, this is a matter for negotiation in the industrial councils but in the Black areas, i.e. the Bantu homelands, the only limits to the advancement of Black workers are the rate at which industries can be established there and at which the Black workers can be trained in the necessary skills.

Both general and technical education and training for the various population groups are well catered for, so that the labour force is continually upgraded to take advantage of improved earnings opportunities. General primary and secondary education for Whites are provided by the four provincial authorities, for Blacks in their homelands by the respective homeland governments, and for Coloureds and Asians by their respective representative councils. A Department of National Education is responsible for technical education and training for Whites, a Department of Bantu Education for general primary and secondary education for Blacks outside their homelands as well as for technical education and training for Blacks, and Departments of Indian and of Coloured Affairs for such education and training facilities for those two population groups as have not yet been transferred to their respective representative councils. Besides taking direct responsibility for technical education and training through these various channels, the government also encourages employers to develop training programmes for their workers by the granting of tax incentives, subsidisation of instructors' salaries, provision of testing facilities, and so on.

The levels of earnings of even the lowest-paid, least skilled of South Africa's population groups, viz. the Blacks, which were referred to above, compare favourably with average earnings levels in other African countries, providing evidence of the relatively advanced level of development already achieved by the South African economy compared to other economies in Africa. For example, in the latest year for which comparable data is available in United Nations sources for some other African countries, viz. 1971, average annual earnings per worker in manufacturing amounted to $291 in Malawi and $357 in Sierra Leone compared to $940 for Black workers in South Africa. It is not surprising, therefore, that in addition to its indigenous labour force, South Africa also attracts large numbers of Black workers from other African countries on a migratory basis. At the beginning of 1973, for example, almost 80 per cent of the gold mining industry's Black labour force of 410 000 were such foreign workers.

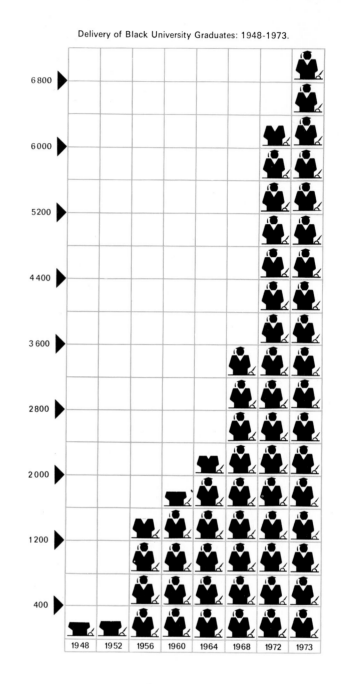

Delivery of Black University Graduates: 1948-1973.

Economic Policy

As in most western countries today, the principal objectives of economic policy in South Africa can be said to be the maintenance of a high level of employment and of a high and stable rate of economic growth; a stable price level; equilibrium in the international balance of payments; and the narrowing of unacceptable income differences, in particular between the country's main population groups.

In the pursuit of these various objectives, the South African authorities have as far as possible made use of indirect policy measures in preference to direct measures which could have the effect of disrupting the workings of the market mechanism, and which are therefore only applied in exceptional instances. Thus, in pursuing a high level of employment and a stable price level, recourse is taken in the first instance to conventional fiscal and monetary policy measures rather than to such drastic inter-

ventions as prices and incomes policies, although in certain critical sectors of the economy selective price controls – not price freezes – are also applied. Similarly, the selective use of import tariffs is explicitly preferred to quantitative import controls as a means of stimulating industrial development, and the determination of wages and working conditions is left as far as possible to collective bargaining procedures within a statutory framework laid down by the government. However, for those parts of the labour force not covered by such collective bargaining procedures, provision is made for periodic minimum wage determinations on a sectoral basis by a statutory Wage Board.

Social services are handled in a similar way, with their provision left in the first instance to private initiative but with the government stepping in to look after the interests of sections of the population who cannot be adequately catered for by private interests. Thus, the provision of housing is financed in the first instance through private building societies, i.e., specialised financial institutions that mobilise funds for this purpose, but the government also operates a National Housing Fund to finance housing for lower-income sections of the population. Similarly, the operation of pension funds is in the first instance the responsibility of employers, within a statutory framework designed to safeguard the interests of contributors, but state pensions are also granted to needy persons who cannot, for various reasons, draw benefits from such private funds.

Although, as became apparent elsewhere, there are a number of state-owned industrial undertakings in South Africa, none of these have come about through nationalisation, or on ideological grounds. In each case there were specific reasons why private entrepreneurs did not wish to, or did not have the resources required to initiate these enterprises, which were nevertheless considered as essential for the balanced development of the economy.

From all this it is evident that economic policy in South Africa takes as its point of departure an economic system that operates on the principle of private business initiative, tempered only by such a degree of government intervention as is considered necessary to overcome the shortcomings of a purely free-enterprise economic system.

Aid to Africa

If it is considered that some 35 per cent of South Africa's total population is still living in areas which must be characterised as underdeveloped, and where the South African government is engaged in vast programmes of economic upliftment, it is rather surprising to find that South Africa is also engaged in development aid outside her own borders.

The main emphasis in South Africa's aid programme to African countries is not in the field financial aid, but nevertheless a Loan Fund for the Promotion of Economic Co-operation was established in 1968. Apart from development loans from this fund, specific contributions to development projects in African countries have been made from time to time by the South African government, as in the case of a $3 million loan to the government of Malawi to help finance the building of a new capital at Lilongwe. The Industrial Development Corporation of South Africa has also made several investments in development projects in African countries, among the largest of which have been a $19 million loan for the development of mining in Botswana and a $16 million loan towards the building of a railway line from Mpinde in Malawi to Nova Freixo in Mozambique. Besides these government and semi-government loans, private South African financial houses have also made several important investments of a developmental nature in a number of African countries.

However, the main thrust of South Africa's contribution in the field of development aid lies in the provision of technical and administrative assistance, for which South Africa is eminently qualified by virtue of the similarity in conditions prevailing there and in other African countries.

In the field of agriculture, for example, South Africa has put her well-developed marketing channels for such commodities as meat, tobacco, bananas, and wool at the disposal of her neighbour states, viz. Lesotho, Botswana, and Swaziland. Technical aid in the agricultural field also takes the form of assistance with pest and disease control measures, the donation of breeding stock, and the dissemination of research results and expertise through the Southern African Regional Commission for the Utilisation of the Soil.

In the area of health, South Africa's highly sophisticated medical research and clinical facilities are at the disposal of neighbouring countries when needed, and assistance in the training of health personnel is regularly given. Several private South African business organisations also sponsor regular working visits to hospitals in neighbouring countries by teams of highly trained medical specialists, who make their services available on a voluntary basis.

Electric power generating systems in the small neighbouring countries have been afforded the benefit of linking up with South Africa's extensive system, thus assuring them of much more dependable supplies of power than they would be able to achieve on their own. South Africa has also expressed her willingness to buy surplus amounts of electricity generated in these countries from plants which cannot be economically justified on the basis of their own domestic demands for electricity.

Other fields in which African countries make regular use of South African facilities and expertise are in transportation, tourism, scientific and industrial research and standardisation. Specialist administrative personnel are also seconded by the South African government to African countries on request, and similarly South African business concerns have made experienced personnel available to get development projects going in neighbouring countries.

Although the nature of these various ways of extending development aid does not allow for ready quantification, and South Africa's aid contribution may therefore not appear impressive besides those of some much larger developed countries, it will be evident from the above instances that South Africa is not shirking its duty of sharing the benefits of her own economic development with other African countries.

SELECT BIBLIOGRAPHY

GENERAL

1. AFRICAN INTERNATIONAL PUB-
LISHERS:
South African Mosaic. Johannesburg: AIPC,
1973. 143p. photos.

2. NIDDRIE, David L.:
South Africa: Nation or Nations? New Jersey:
Von Nostrand, 1968. 176p. illus. bibl.

3. HARRIGAN, Anthony:
The New Republic – South Africa's role in the
world. Pretoria: Van Schaik, 1966. 94p.

4. BULPIN, Thomas Victor:
Discovering South Africa. Cape Town: Books
of Africa, 1970. 785p. illus., maps, photos.

5. TYACK, Maurice:
South Africa, Land of Challenge. Lausanne:
France Inter Presse, 1970. 404p. photos.

6. LE GUÈBE, Jacques:
L'Afrique du Sud. Paris: de Duca, 1974. 376p.

7. GINIEWSKI, Paul:
Une Autre Afrique du Sud. Paris: Editions
Berger-Levrault. 312p. photos.

8. LA REVUE FRANCAISE:
Edition spéciale sur l'Afrique du Sud, Juin 1970.
Numéro spécial sur la République d'Afrique
du Sud, Avril 1973. Paris.

9. HOLM, Erik:
Tier und Gott: Mythik, Mantik and Magie der
Südafrikanischen Urjäger. Basel: Schwabe,
1965. 198p. illus.

10. HOLM, Erik:
Die Felsbilder Südafrikas: Deutung und Bedeu-
tung. Tübingen: Wasmuth, (c 1969). 131p.
illus., maps.

11. ZUR STRASSEN, Helmut:
Land zwischen zwei Wüsten. Cape Town:
Purnell, 1971. 150p. illus. maps.

12. HARTMANN, Hans:
Südafrika: Geschichte – Wirtschaft – Politik.
Stuttgart: W. Kohlhammer, (c 1968). 158p.
map.

HISTORY

1. KRUGER, Rayne:
Goodbye Dolly Gray; the story of the Boer War.
London: Four Square, 1964. 512p. maps.

2. KRUGER, Daniël Wilhelmus:
The Making of a Nation: a history of the Union
of South Africa, 1910–1961. Johannesburg:
Macmillan, 1969. 348p. illus., maps. bibl.

3. MULLER, Christoffel Frederik Jakobus, ed.:
500 Years: A History of South Africa. Pretoria:
Academica, 1968. 489p. maps. bibl.

4. VERWOERD, Hendrik Frensch:
Verwoerd Speaks – Speeches 1948–1962; edited
by A. N. Pelzer, Johannesburg: APB Publishers,
1966. 676p.

5. LACOUR-GAYET, Robert:
Histoire de l'Afrique du Sud. Paris: Fayard,
1970. 487p. maps. bibl.

PEOPLE

1. FISHER, John:
The Afrikaners. London: Cassell, 1969. 380p.
plates. maps. bibl.

2. SCHAPERA, Isac, ed.:
The Bantu Speaking Tribes of South Africa.
Cape Town: Maskew Miller, 1962. 453p. maps.
photos.

3. ELLIOT, Aubrey:
The Magic World of the Xhosa. Johannesburg:
Collins, 1970.

4. BECKER, Peter:
Peoples of Southern Africa, Johannesburg: The
Star, 1971. 62p. illus., photos.

5. MORRIS, Donald R.:
The Washing of the Spears – a history of the rise
of the Zulu nation under Shaka and its fall in the
Zulu War of 1879. New York: Simon and
Schuster, 1965. 655p. maps. photos.

6. TYRRELL, Barbara:
Tribal Peoples of Southern Africa. Cape Town:
Books of Africa, 1971. 206p. illus. bibl.

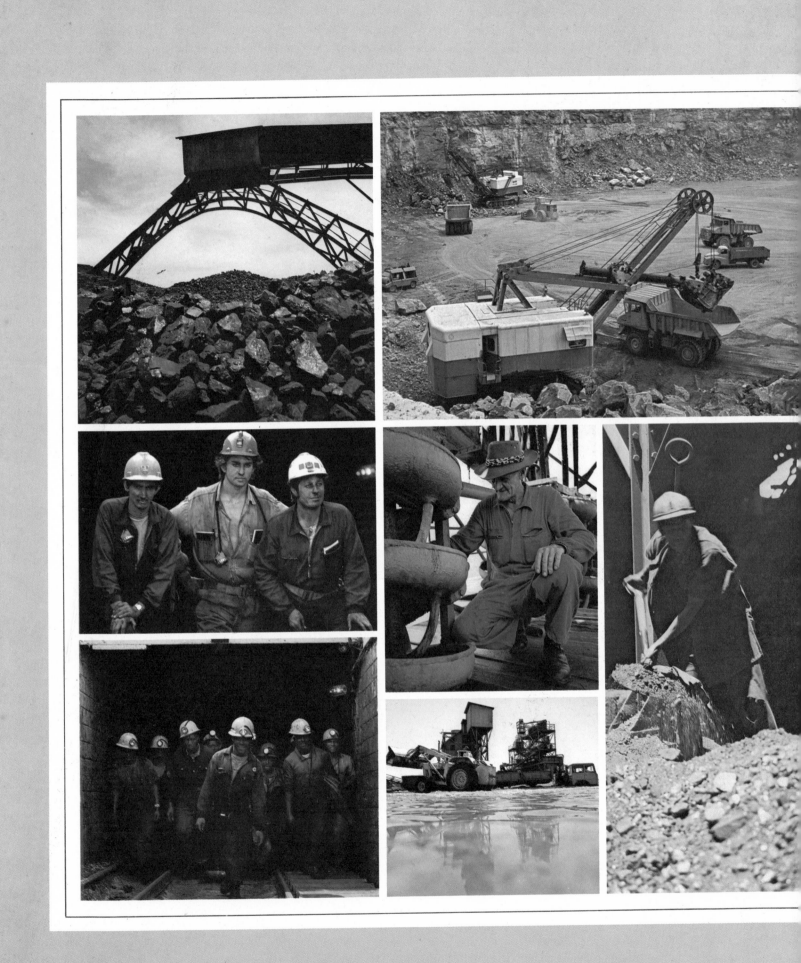

7. DU PLESSIS, Izak David:
   The Malay Quarter and its People. Cape Town: Balkema, 1953. 91p. illus., photos.

POLITICS

1. RHOODIE, Nicolaas Johannes:
   Apartheid and Racial Partnership in Southern Africa. Pretoria: Academica, 1969. 429p. bibl.

2. RHOODIE, Nicolaas Johannes:
   South African Dialogue: contrasts in South African thinking on basic race issues. Johannesburg: McGraw-Hill, 1972. 630p.

3. RHOODIE, Eschel Mostert:
   The Paper Curtain. Johannesburg: Voortrekkerpers. 1969. 212p. bibl.

4. COCKRAM, Gail-Maryse:
   Vorster's Foreign Policy. Pretoria: Academica, 1970. 222p. illus., maps. bibl.

5. WORRALL, Denis, ed.:
   South Africa: Government and Politics. Pretoria: Van Schaik, 1972. 366p.

6. LEJEUNE, Anthony:
   The Case for South West Africa. London: Tom Stacey, 1971. 245p. map. bibl.

7. DE VILLIERS, David:
   The Case for South Africa. London: Tom Stacey, 1970. 156p.

8. DEPARTMENT OF INFORMATION:
   The Reality of Multi-National Development in South Africa. Pretoria, 1974. 180p. tables. maps.

9. BARRATT, John:
   Accelerated Development in Southern Africa, by John Barratt, Simon Brand, David S. Collier and Kurt Glaser. London: Macmillan, 1974. 706p.

10. GINIEWSKI, Paul:
    Livre Noir, Livre Blanc. Paris: Editions Berger-Levrault, 1966, 256p. maps.

11. JENNY, Hans:
    Africa kommt nicht mit leeren Händen. Stuttgart: Kohlhammer, 1971. 279p. graphs. maps.

12. ZIESEL, Kurt:
    Schwarz und Weiss in Afrika. München: J.F. Lehmanns Verlag, 1973. 144p. map. photos.

ECONOMICS

1. HOUGHTON, D. Hobart:
   The South African Economy. Cape Town: University Press, 1972. 280p. diagrs. graphs. map. bibl.

2. DE FREITAS, Frank, ed.:
   Industrial Profile of South Africa. Johannesburg: Da Gama. 114p. maps. photos.

3. AFRIKAANSE HANDELSINSTITUUT:
   South African Progress 1972, edited by D.J. Greyling. Pretoria. 1969 – (biennially). 184p. photos.

4. LOMBARD, Johannes Anthonie:
   The Concept of Economic Co-operation in Southern Africa, by J. A. Lombard, J. J. Stadler and P. J. van der Merwe. Pretoria: Econburo, 1968. 72p. map.

5. AGENCE ECONOMIQUE ET FINANCIERE
   Republique d'Afrique du Sud. Paris, October 1971.

6. CHRIS VAN RENSBURG PUBLICATIONS:
   Homelands: The Role of the Corporations. Johannesburg, 1974. 244p. tables. maps. photos.

7. CHRIS VAN RENSBURG PUBLICATIONS:
   Decentralisation – Growth Points 1974. Johannesburg, 1974. 440p. tables. map.

8. DA GAMA PUBLISHERS:
   Workshop of a Continent. Johannesburg, 1974. 200p. illus. photos.

YEARBOOKS, ANNUALS AND ENCYCLOPAEDIAS

1. DEPARTMENT OF INFORMATION:
   Official Yearbook of the Republic of South Africa. Pretoria, 1974. plates. maps. photos bibl.

2. ROSENTHAL, Eric, comp. and ed.:
   Encyclopaedia of Southern Africa. 6th edition 1973. London: Warne, 1961, 662p. illus., maps. photos.

3. NASOU:
   Standard Encyclopaedia of Southern Africa. Cape Town, 1970. V. plates. illus., maps. photos.

4. DE KOCK, Willem Johannes: ed.:
   Dictionary of South African Biography. Cape Town: Nasionale Boekhandel, 1968. v.

5. ALBERTYN, W., ed.:
   Official South African Municipal Yearbook. Pretoria: South African Association of Municipal Employees.

6. NATIONAL PUBLISHING COMPANY:
   Advertising and Press Annual of Africa. Johannesburg.

7. S.A. MINING JOURNAL SYNDICATE:
   S.A. Mining and Engineering Yearbook. v illus., maps.

8. BEERMAN'S FINANCIAL YEARBOOK OF SOUTHERN AFRICA:
   Investor's Manual and Encyclopaedia of South African Public Companies. Johannesburg: Combined Publishers. 2v.

9. VISUAL PUBLICATIONS:
   South Africa: A Visual History 1973. Johannesburg: Perskor, 1973. 156p.